America in Decline

America in Decline

How the Loss of Civic Virtue and Standards of Excellence Is Causing the End of Pax Americana

Justin P. DePlato
Alex C. Minford

LEXINGTON BOOKS
Lanham • Boulder • New York • London

Published by Lexington Books
An imprint of The Rowman & Littlefield Publishing Group, Inc.
4501 Forbes Boulevard, Suite 200, Lanham, Maryland 20706
www.rowman.com

86-90 Paul Street, London EC2A 4NE, United Kingdom

British Library Cataloguing in Publication Information Available

Library of Congress Cataloging-in-Publication Data Available

ISBN 9781793627513 (cloth) | ISBN 9781793627520 (ebook)

Contents

Introduction

The American Republic is in the midst of change, which formally began about three decades ago. Leadership, specifically at the national level, has sharply declined—America's leaders are less genuine, honest, and ethical. Rather than examining individual members of Congress, in which there would be plenty of examples to draw from, an analysis of the Presidents of the United States will suffice. The Presidents of today are monumentally different from the early Presidents, who were not only great politicians, but also revered citizens.

George Washington was a Revolutionary War hero; John Adams championed legal representation rights; Thomas Jefferson wrote the Declaration of Independence and helped to end the slave trade in Virginia; James Madison combed through thousands of years of political philosophy to create the U.S. Constitution; and James Monroe ushered in a new period of international relations that was founded on American strength. Other great leaders in American history, such as Abraham Lincoln, Franklin D. Roosevelt, Dwight D. Eisenhower, John F. Kennedy, and Ronald Reagan were not only loved and celebrated, but revered for their intelligence, charisma, and leadership ability. These presidents did not happen by accident—they were the result of a populace that possessed their same qualities.

Within the past three decades, however, U.S. presidents have declined in all three of the above facets: Bill Clinton was caught performing sexual acts with an intern in the Oval Office, George W. Bush was infamous for saying nonsensical quotes in press conferences and barely being able to complete sentences, Barack Obama tarnished the global reputation of the U.S. by instituting weakness as a foreign policy, and Donald Trump has been caught saying at least twenty lies per day, for which he is cheered by his electorate. The leadership in our country from the 1990s to the 2010s has been atrocious, which is responsible for the declining lack of civic virtue in society. This logically follows if one accepts the premise that an electorate will imitate the characteristics of their leaders, which has been accepted since the days of Thomas Hobbes. Eventually, the degeneration of civic virtue got so bad that the citizenry embodied a general lack of morality, intelligence, and even decency. At that point, the country elected an absolute demagogue, President Donald Trump.

Since the days of his infamous election, political scientists have quickly attempted to explain the election of Trump. The theories ranged from Trump being elected due to Russian election interference, which was pushed by the Democratic Party, to Trump being a revolution against the establishment, which was pushed by the Republican Party. Both theories are wrong. Today in society, there are rising obesity rates, higher drop-out rates, increased viewership of pornographic material, increased drug and alcohol abuse, and less trust between neighbors. In 2016, the people elected a man to the White House who literally embodies all of these things. Trump has foregone any attempt to keep himself healthy, has cheated on his wife with a porn star, has repeatedly lied to his base at rallies, has consistently attacked political adversaries and journalists like a child on social media, and has failed to display a genuine trust in anyone other than himself. In conclusion, if people want to know why Trump has risen to power, they need only look into a mirror.

As a result of the citizenry's lack of civic virtue and apparent intransigence, the country is now descending into a partisan war zone. People are more likely to identify as a Republican or Democrat than as an American. The only way to prevent the country from deteriorating further is for the citizenry to improve itself, which will naturally manifest better leaders. Eventually, if the people expect more from themselves, the leaders will follow suit, and the country will revert back to a state of common morality and peaceful discourse.

Lastly, it should be noted that we do not appear in support of either political party—we are concerned with helping the American Republic, not the Democrats or Republicans. In the end, the only hope lies with you, the People. If the system is not corrected soon, the country will reach an irreparable level from which there is no return. Only posterity shall determine whether our warning was heeded. Therefore, do with this work as you choose.

> "Our Constitution was made only for a moral and religious people. It is wholly inadequate to the government of any other."—John Adams, 1798

Chapter 1

Civic Virtue in Greece and Rome

There are several giants in the realm of political theory who created governments more than capable of working, and even thriving. Plato's kallipolis, Aristotle's polity, Augustine's theocracy, Hobbes's kingship, and even Marx's communism all have a place in the conversation of the "political good life." Their contributions to justice, authority, ethics, and education have transcended the field for hundreds, even thousands, of years. Better yet, they will continue to demand interest and attention for years to come. This work, however, will focus primarily on three societies: Ancient Greece, Rome, and the United States. With reference to Greece, we will evaluate the two major city-states of Athens and Sparta. With reference to Rome, we will evaluate both the Republic and the Empire. Each society carried unique expectations of citizenship, which can be illustrated through the analysis of their governmental systems. Finally, we will discuss how the morals, ethics, and cultures of Greece and Rome formed a foundation of the pursuit of excellence and civic virtue, which was utilized by the Founders to establish the principles in the early United States.

ATHENS

We will begin with the ancient city of Athens, known for being the world's first democracy. Democracy derives from the word "demokratia," which translates to "the people rule." Its roots in Athens can be traced back to 507 BC.[1] At first, it began as a series of reforms by Cleisthenes, who was an ancient lawmaker in Athens. Although people today, even around the globe, assume democracy to be commonplace, at the time this was an extremely revolutionary idea. The rest of the Greek city-states were either monarchies, timocracies, or oligarchies. The majority of these states were monarchical, meaning the city had an established class system, with the ruler being a King, or sometimes referred to as a Sovereign. Far less common was the timocracy, which is a government based on honor; typically, this is a military society where the patriarch is the military leader. The common example of this type of government was the city of Sparta. Then, of course, there was the oligarchy, a society based on wealth where only property holders possess political power. Despite their neighbors restricting freedom from the citizenry, Athens stood proud in the face of change.

The Athenians instituted three branches to their new system of direct democracy: the ekklesia, the boule, and the dikasteria. The first branch, the ekklesia, was the governing body which made laws. However, rather than having representatives, or diplomats, any of the city's 40,000 men could attend the sessions. This is a system of direct democracy, where everybody has a say in the laws being passed or negated. The boule was the manifestation of ten different Athenian tribes, and formed a council of representatives. In total, there were 500 men, 50 from each tribe. These people controlled foreign policy as well as the oversight of government operations. The last branch was the dikasteria, which was a court comprised of ordinary citizens; almost 500 jurors—over the age of 30were chosen every day to rule on cases brought forth by the demos. This court was commonly renowned as the most important institution. As Herodotus, a Greek historian, wrote: "In a democracy, there is, first, that most splendid of virtues, equality before the law." These three branches combined to create the first democratic experiment in the history of humanity.

To understand the expectation of civic virtue, we have to discuss the advantages and disadvantages to this system. Democracy, as previously stated, was a fresh idea, but it was also a popular one amongst the citizens of Athens. The first advantage of direct democracy is that it creates an equal playing field—all people, regardless of race, gender, ethnicity, wealth, or any other factor, are seen as equals, and all contribute collectively to the executive, legislative, and judicial processes.[2] In this way, the society does not become the game board for the elites; rather, the poor man is just as powerful as the rich man, for their votes carry the same weight. Another advantage is that society reaches a perfect level of congeniality. When there is an expectation within a city that everyone is to be involved in the governmental processes, there exists a level of trust between the people, and a shared common goal for the community. Today, this responsibility is referred to as "civic duty," and it was a cornerstone of Athens.

For the first century or so, Athenian democracy flourished, accomplishing wonders. It soon became the western epicenter of mathematics, science, and philosophy. Also, it was on the cusp of technological advance. Athens became the pinnacle of intelligence and knowledge. Socrates, the teacher of Plato, founded the School of Athens, which was a center for philosophy and science. The goal of the Athenians was to become enlightened, which was thought possible through scientific inquiry and wisdom. Socrates, Plato, and Aristotle were political giants, who debated and wrote their own blueprints for the perfect governmental systems. In Athens, politics was linked closely with ethics and virtue. However, the impact of the city transcended politics and law. Euclid of Alexandria is known as the "Father of Geometry," Archimedes was the ancient equivalent of Albert Einstein in physics, and Hipparchus of Nicaea discovered the elliptical pattern of the Earth around the Sun. Athens was also the major hub for medical advancement, and medical students in the world today still learn about the standards of ethics created by Hippocrates in fifth century B.C.

The standards of excellence in Athens can be summarized by analyzing Aristotle's *The Nicomachean Ethics*. Aristotle dedicated the work to Nicomachus, his son—the goal was to teach his son exactly what was expected of him in society. Among the most famous lines of the book is when Aristotle writes, "One swallow does not make a summer . . . We are what we repeatedly do. Excellence, then, is not an act but a habit." The expectation of excellence and virtue set forth by Aristotle is mirrored by Epicurus, who argued that through "sober reasoning," people can gain pleasure by obtaining knowledge. Thomas Jefferson later stated in a letter to William Short in 1819 that he identified himself as an Epicurean. The Athenians did not just advocate for ethical excellence, but rather excellence of entirety. This Greek city-state was the first to create athletic competition, which took place in Olympia. The members of the School of Athens recognized that in a direct democracy, excellence is the key. Therefore, citizens should be excellent in all facets: diversified in knowledge, physically fit, honest and reliable, and active members of the society. Happiness, or Eudaimonia, was achieved in Athens through being excellent in every conceived capacity.

As the second century of the society's reign approached, the democracy began to degenerate due to the decline of civic virtue and excellence in the society. Basic foundations were crippled, and institutions collapsed, which allowed for the city's fall in 338 B.C. by King Philip II of Macedonia. The near-divine Athenian democratic experiment, the once shimmering utopia of the west, eventually fell to bloodshed and despair. However, this was not by accident—civic virtue collapsed, which highlighted the inherent problems with direct democracy itself.

Most people, especially Americans, are taught that democracy is the greatest political system of all time. To the contrary, if not well-protected by the populace, it becomes exposed to problems that can, and almost certainly will, lead to a country's peril. We will next explore the problems with democracies, and why they tend to always destroy themselves.

PROBLEMS WITH DEMOCRACY

On December 17, 1814, John Adams wrote in a letter to John Taylor, where he exclaimed, "Remember, democracy never lasts long. It soon wastes, exhausts, and murders itself. There never was a democracy yet that did not commit suicide."[3] Amongst political philosophers, there is a mutual consensus that democracy is not an effective system, but why? There are three main reasons why democracy will inevitably fail in any society: 1) the system allows for the formation of factions, which deteriorate the loyalty citizens have to the state, 2) once standards of excellence decline and citizens are no longer pursuing intellectual growth, policy decisions will be made by an unintelligent and fickle population, and 3) political and societal institutions will be disparaged if a citizenry abandons all attempts to compromise, which will ensue mob rule. First, we will examine how the formation of factions can be destructive to a society, and why faction formation is likely.

The term faction, in an American sense, is famous from James Madison's *Federalist No. 10,* in which he describes a faction as a group of people "who are united and actuated by some common impulse of passion, or of interest, adverse to the rights of other citizens, or to the permanent and aggregate interests of the community."[4] In other words, a faction is nothing more than a special interest group. However, for them to have a detrimental effect on democracy, they also have to be inevitable, that is, if only some groups of people form factions and others do not, then it is not evidence towards democracy's demise. Therefore, our inquiry must turn towards human nature. Do humans seek to conform or differentiate? If all people seek to differentiate, then there can never be universality of thought or action; thus, factions will always form.

In a psychological study by Daniel Wegner, he picked random people and told them not to think about a white bear.[5] He then proceeded to give each of them five minutes to think aloud. If the participant thought or spoke "white bear" then they would have to ring a bell. On average, the participants uttered the phrase once or twice in the five minutes, and it appeared in their thoughts every minute. However, to make matters worse, when the five-minute period ended, they thought about white bears more than twice as much as those who had been specifically instructed to think about them. The study was repeated three times, and the results repeated themselves, creating a verifiable conclusion—people tend to think about things they are not supposed to think about, and do things they are instructed not to do. This is a trait of all humans, and the problem may be worse for Americans, due to the country's specific origin of rebellion from Great Britain.

There is another example of this, but one which is far more humorous. Based on the amount of Republican representation per district, taking into account the size of the state and its population, the most conservative states in the U.S. are Louisiana, Mississippi, and Alabama. These states are considered the "deep south," and have not gone blue (in favor of the Democratic Party) in a presidential election since 1976. The people in these states who align with that paradigm preach traditional conservative values. Therefore, the majority of the people in these states who identify as Conservatives also oppose both same-sex marriage and the acceptance of homosexuality in society, citing it violates Judeo-Christian values.[6] However, the most interesting data point comes from an industry not usually mentioned in the world of academia—pornography. According to Business Insider, the largest proportion of gay porn viewers in the U.S. comes from Louisiana, Mississippi, and Alabama.[7] Seems a bit oxymoronic. So, by the day these citizens are rallying outside churches with signs that read "Gays go to Hell," but at night they are embracing their own homosexual desires. While this topic is not one typically appropriate for academia, it acknowledges that people frequently differentiate themselves from societal standards.

We have found that people are likely to differentiate both from others and from society at older ages, but what about the younger population? A counterargument to my analysis, so far, could potentially be that if education can instill communal ideas in children, rather than individualism, the direct democracy could still be salvaged. Schools, then, are the best determinant for testing this hypothesis. Consider this article entitled: "What do kids think about school uniforms?"[8]

Kids love to experiment with their clothing and accessories; a student's

> apparel is an extension of their personality. People say you only get one chance to make a first impression, and for kids, clothing is an important part of that first impression. Kids often feel constricted by the rules and regulations of the classrooms, and school uniforms only further emphasize that restricted feeling. As Maryam, age nine, points out on Discovery Girls: "Sometimes clothes can show your emotions and expression . . . *and you should be happy you're different*."

In total, the numbers speak for themselves. According to Scholastic, in a study involving 2,943 middle and high school students from all different regions in the U.S., only 560 of them were in support of school uniforms.[9] This means that out of the sample, more than 80% opposed a dress code. Clearly, then, children seek to differentiate themselves from others too. Therefore, a basic truth of human nature, as Machiavelli predicted in *The Prince*, is that people seek differentiation from others. Therefore, they want their customs, traditions, beliefs, forms of self-expression, and their political ideas to be unique.

In order to obtain this objective, individuals must retain a sense of personal sovereignty, which implies occasionally diverting from the norms of society.

To summarize, human nature ensures that people are unlikely to conform with others or with society. If one objectively analyzes the world from a realist perspective, then this idea gains validity. Nobody, at least in the American sense, is raised to think about other people. People do not give up their own property, wealth, or ideas to others without receiving subsequent compensation, and are likely to rebel against societal constraints. More so, people look more inwardly towards themselves, and attempt to be different than the surrounding population. It seems, then, that Machiavelli was correct—in *The Prince*, he stated that people differentiate themselves naturally from other people in order to gain dominion, and they will manipulate and deceive others if need be. Therefore, human nature is to differentiate, which means that factions are inevitable in any society. Once factions form, the loyalty to the state is diminished, as citizens as pitted against one another. Again, we can use the mighty Athens as a prime example.

The decline of loyalty to the state, in accordance with the degradation of civic virtue, caused the society to slip into a polarized and partisan war zone. One of the best historical accounts of the fall of Athens comes from the historian Thucydides, who wrote *The Peloponnesian War*. In the book, he describes the final moments of the Athenian democratic experiment:

> Family relations were a weaker tie than party membership, since party members were more ready to go to any extreme for any reason. These parties were not formed to enjoy the benefit of the established laws, but to acquire power by overthrowing the existing regime; and the members of these parties felt confidence in each other not because of any fellowship in a religious or societal communion, but because they were partners in crime.[10]

Thucydides gracefully provided us with the answer to our question: factions are destructive because they shift the allegiance of the citizenry away from the country and towards the party. The minority party, the one not currently in power, would rather see the country fail under the majority party just to prove a point than to see their own country succeed under people they detest. This attitude destroys the congeniality of the society, which diminishes the trust between different people. One of the principles of excellence under Plato was to have trust in the leaders of a society. In *The Republic*, Plato argues that the kallipolis will only thrive if the Producers and Auxiliaries align directly with the vision set forth for the society by the Guardians, or Philosopher Kings. As a result of factions, the vision for the country divides itself into different directions, which causes the downfall of social, ethical, and moral commonality. Progressing the society forward without a unified direction is like sailing into the eye of a hurricane with cracks in the hull of the ship—it will sink.

Recall that the second problem with democracy is that once standards of excellence decline and citizens are no longer pursuing intellectual growth, policy decisions will be made by an unintelligent and fickle population. Since the people of Athens voted directly on all matters, it was imperative to make academic enlightenment the cornerstone of the society. In Plato's Theory of the Forms, he suggests that there are good versions of all things. Under common scheme or plan, one could extend that to say that there exists good policies and bad ones, and if the populace declines in intelligence, it is a certainty that poor policy will be made.

Pretend, for a moment, that you are a parent, with a partner, in a household which has four children. Our model in this case is the household, which would be the government, and it is operated like a direct democracy. One day, you hold a vote to see what the entire family should eat for breakfast. Both you and the other partner suggest eggs, or maybe cereal. However, the children, being the young age that they are, want ice cream for breakfast. Under a democratic system, the children would win, because four votes defeat two. The next day, the same vote would repeat itself, and so on. Even though the parents are old enough to understand the dangers of the children eating ice cream every morning for breakfast, including the vast health complications it could cause, they are powerless to stop it. An ancient Greek proverb once said, "You believe democracy works? Try it in your own household." The Athenians fell victim to this paradox in their own society, as people began to make financial policies intended to aid the lower classes and create safety nets. Given the structure of their market, the city-state did not have the capital or revenue stream to support such a proposal, which prevented economic growth. The lack of economic growth was one main contributing factor to Athens' defeat against Sparta in 404 B.C. at the conclusion of the Peloponnesian War.

The Athenians, especially those located around the School of Athens, always valued education, as it was the key to progress and enlightenment. In Plato's Allegory of the Cave, he argues that all people are born with instincts that are contrary to maintaining a civil society:

> Like ourselves, I replied; and they see only their own shadows, or the shadows of one another, which the fire throws on the opposite wall of the cave. And suppose further that the prison had an echo which came from the other side, would they not be sure to fancy when one of the passers-by spoke that the voice which they heard came from the passing shadow?

The argument of Plato through the allegory is to prove that human beings are born with instincts, not intelligence. Without education, humans would maintain their ignorance, that is, people would stay in the safety of the cave—another way of saying, ignorance is bliss. However, through education, humans can leave the cave and discover the truth to governance, ethics, justice, science, and mathematics. In Athens, as the end of their society loomed, the citizens, according to Thucydides, began to use political arguments predicated on emotion and feeling rather than logic and reason.

The last reason for the fall of democracies is that political and societal institutions will be disparaged if the citizenry abandons all attempts to compromise, resulting in mob rule. Without an educated populace, poor policy decisions will manifest. Throughout history, these poor policies could be of the political, social, economic, or military nature—it does not really matter the specific area of the policy, the effect will be the same. As the society degenerates, turmoil created from the effects of poor policy exacerbates the factions, and they begin ruthlessly fighting for power. Among the first traits the society will lose are moral values, respect for authority, and an obedience and adherence to the rule of law. Once society abandons its principles, the social fabric has been forever altered, upon which it is increasingly difficult to revert. The mob will then attempt to obtain government control, and should they succeed in doing so, they will coerce action through force, and the society is left in ruins. Thus, the only legitimate results are civil war amongst the factions, total annihilation from a foreign enemy since the society is not able to coordinate an effective defense, or the rise of a tyrant and demagogue who claims to be a savior.

The three resulting outcomes of a democracy's decline have been well documented throughout world history, and all of the instances have been the culmination of a lack of civic virtue in the societies. In 1665, as the Congo gained its independence from Belgium, competing factions became so hostile that a civil war arose, which became known as the Kongo Civil War. When Athens suffered from the result of democratic collapse, they were unable to coordinate a defense against Philip II in 338 B.C., which ensured the city's destruction. Finally, when the Weimar Republic faced an economic depression, the democracy fell, which gave rise to Adolf Hitler and the Nazi Party in 1934—Hitler rose from the ashes as the savior of Germany.

We have discussed the history of Athens and how the decline of civic virtue caused its democratic collapse. Now we will analyze the government and culture of Sparta, the other famous city-state of Ancient Greece.

SPARTA

Sparta was a southern city-state in the Ancient Greek superpower. Although it existed as a society for around 1,000 years, we are going to focus on its civilization from 464 B.C. to 371 B.C. In 464 B.C., it was destroyed by an earthquake, so the society was forced to rebuild, and they also adjusted some societal and political norms that were proving problematic. The society existed for nearly a century until it was conquered in 464 B.C. in the Battle of Leuctra. Even though the reign of Sparta was numerically inferior to Athens, it is still known today as one of the strongest and most prosperous Greek city-states, which warrants analysis.

The government of Sparta was extremely unique for its time. As previously discussed, Athens was a direct democracy, which was centered around excellence, ethics, and intellectual ability. In Sparta, however, intellectual ability and progressivism was not highly regarded. Rather, it was a timocracy, which is a society centered around honor and loyalty to the state. Specifically, their timocratic government possessed monarchical and oligarchical roots. According to Hans Beck's *A Companion to Ancient Greek Government*, the main leaders of their executive branch were two kings, both deriving from the Agiad and Eurypontid families. The kings, during war time, were the main commanders of Sparta's army, and during peace time had a variety of functions in the judicial branch for tribunals. The legislative functions were carried out by the Gerousia, which was a Council of Elders, primarily Senators and Gerontocrats. The Elders were above the law in every sense, and they were not held accountable to their actions or words, in typical oligarchical fashion. The Apella was a national assembly designed to maintain social authority, and primarily consisted of both military members and retired military members. For each tribe in Sparta, there were five separate advisors, called Ephors, and the oldest of the five was known as the *magistrate eponymos*. The Ephors did not kneel before the kings, but rather were held in high societal regard—they were essentially the priests of religious practices.

The government of Sparta was designed, through their Constitution, so that the Kings would have the majority of the power during times of conflict, when the civilization received threats and acts of aggression from foreign powers, which included other Greek city-states. The concentration of power in the Executive Branch was by design—Sparta was predominantly a military society. Every male was required to become a member of the military until the age of thirty, when they could choose to go into the political arena or stay in the military. All common labor in the society was accomplished through a slave labor force, called the Helots. Given their governmental structure, and the norms of the society, there were specific citizenship expectations.

Men and women in Sparta were not treated equally, but both served a useful function. As George Chryssikos stated in *Ancient Sparta: The Home of Constitutional Government*, women in Sparta received far more freedoms than they would in other Greek city-states. Although they could not vote on legislative matters, nor on military strategy, they were highly respected for their role in maintaining the integrity of households. They were also used frequently as being the symbols of fidelity and beauty. The legend is that the Spartans were descendant from Hercules, and women considered it a privilege to birth Spartan men. After a male child was born, he was evaluated by the government. Any child who was not apparently healthy was cast out of the society. If a female child was healthy, she was raised in the household under the mother; if a male child was healthy, he was raised until he gained initial motor function, at which point he was given to the military for training, which typically began as young as six years old. Spartan men prided themselves as being the military elite. The entire population of men were well-trained warriors. Stephen Hodkinson wrote in *Sparta & War* that soldiers considered giving their life for Sparta to be the "highest honor" they could achieve in their life.

The citizenship expectation in Sparta was to have an eternal loyalty to the state, and to act at all times with honor, never deviating from the orders given by the Kings. The end goal of one's life was to obtain glory, which was not terribly difficult considering that soldiers in any military intervention were prohibited, by Spartan law, to retreat or surrender. Even when facing insurmountable odds, the warrior-elite were required to stand and fight, to the death. The conviction of Spartan soldiers gave the entire society a fierce reputation throughout all of Greece, and many of their traditions and philosophies form the basis for modern-day military practice.

The most notable instance of Sparta's power and perseverance came when Persian forces descended on Greece. To maintain Greek autonomy, a force of 300 Spartans and another 7,000 Greeks, mostly Macedonians, were led by King Leonidas I against the Achaemenid Empire of Xerxes I, which consisted of upwards of 100,000 men. On September 8, 480 B.C., the Battle of Thermopylae began. For three days, the Spartans led the Greek forces to victory, and they held the line. On the third day of battle, a Persian spy named Ephialtes learned of the Greek strategy and informed the Persians of the plan. As is Spartan law, the soldiers decided to fight until their last breath, and every member of the 300 was killed in battle, including King Leonidas. This story of bravery and duty sparked a fire across all of Greece, which inspired the country to join together to fight the Persians. The combined Greek forces met Xerxes' army one year later at the Battle of Plataea, and the Greeks, led by the entire Spartan army, were victorious.

The military culture of Sparta normally enabled the society to defend itself against any and all foreign threats. Each Spartan, on the battlefield, was roughly equivalent to 5–10 foreign adversaries. However, the advantage of foreign numbers eventually proved too great for Sparta. According to *The Decline of Sparta*, by G. L. Cawkwell, at the Battle of Leuctra, there were only 700 Spartans left, compared to 10,000 Hoplites. Aristotle would later go on to write that the city "was destroyed because of the shortage of manpower," not because of the disintegrated culture of the society. Sparta was a great society, by all metrics. There is an inherent and distinct power in creating a society where the main principles of civic virtue are honor and loyalty to the state. It seems, then, that a powerhouse civilization would be one which combines the lessons of Athens and Sparta—a society that has a high emphasis on education, ethics, and scientific enlightenment, while also having an emphasis on honor and nationalism. Welcome, my friend, to Rome.

ROME

The term "Ancient Rome" actually encompasses two completely different societies: the Roman Republic, and the Roman Empire. For the sake of this work, we will only be analyzing the Roman Republic, due to its overwhelming similarity to the United States. Before the Roman Republic, there was a Kingship in place, which ended in 509 B.C. when the son of the seventh king of Rome, Lucious Tarquinius Superbus, allegedly raped the chaste Lucretia. Due to the scandal, the citizens of Rome demanded a dismantling of the central government, so that no concentration of power would ever exist again. The citizens decided to create the Roman Republic—republic derives from *res publica*, meaning "public thing." From 509 B.C. to 31 B.C., the Roman Republic reigned as the most powerful sovereign state in the world.

To understand the civic virtues present in the Roman Republic, we must first understand its societal norms. First, it is important to note that the society was built upon social classes.[11] The upper class, known as the Patricians, were the elites of the Roman society. The lower class consisted of the common people, what Plato's *Republic* would call the producers, and they were known as the Plebeians. These two social groups were distinct, and they were regularly kept separated from one another within the government and in society– for example, it was illegal for a man and woman of the opposite class to marry. The Patricians were the only class that voted for local magistrates. When these officials retired from the Magistrate, they would frequently join the Roman Senate, the highest legislative body in the Republic. According to Mary Beard's *SPQR: A History of Ancient Rome*, the Senate consisted of 300 elites who oversaw the creation of all laws, specifically those referring to taxation, spending, and foreign relations. The Senators, every year, would elect two Consuls—executive authorities who controlled the military and oversaw the entire government. These Consuls also had the power to veto any motion that the Senate passed.

Furthermore, in the event of an emergency, one of the Consuls would be promoted to Dictator, and would have absolute authority over the entire city until the emergency had concluded. According to Mary Beard, the Plebeians controlled the Assemblies, which were legislative bodies where all people voted on legislative matters (direct democracy). These Assemblies, although numerous, were not as powerful as the Senate, as they had no control over the actual passage of laws for the entire Republic; rather, they would only handle legislative matters that pertained to their own districts, which usually involved financial matters. Over time, according to Andrew Lintott's *The Constitution of the Roman Republic*, the lower class complained about not having any say in the Senate, so the government created a special position, known as the Tribune, which served as the Plebeians' personal representative in the body. This position was selected by the Assemblies, and he had the power to veto any motion passed by the Senate, which became known as the Tribune's veto.

After the Tribune's post was created, ordinary seats in the Senate began to be opened to Plebeians. They even expanded the number of Tribunes to about ten. Approaching the first century B.C.E., according to *SPQR: A History of Ancient Rome*, the Senate grew stagnate: blockades against legislation, caused by constant bickering between the Patricians and Plebeians, rendered the government ineffective. Soon, the numbers in the Senate became nearly equal between the two political parties: the Optimates (Patricians) and the Populares (Plebeians). Having nearly equal say, they each elected a Consul to represent their party (this was the first time the Consuls represented parties rather than Rome itself). The Consul of the Optimates was named Gnaeus Pompey Magnus; the Consul of the Populares was named Gaius Julius Caesar; although they did not hold office at the same time, they were both key leaders during the Roman Republic's collapse.[12] Both known for the heroic actions in conquest, each had a different vision for the future of Rome.

In 50 B.C., Pompey Magnus returned to Rome from his conquest in the Mediterranean while Julius Caesar opted to stay in battle against the northern territories. Although the Populares had enough members in the Senate to elect a Consul, they still lacked a majority. The Optimates, fearing Caesar could become a dictator, demanded that he return to Rome immediately, to which he refused. In response, according to Tom Holland's *Rubicon: The Last Years of the Roman Republic*, the Optimates used their majority in the Senate to pass a motion that declared Caesar an enemy of the state. This action by the Optimates made factions in Rome even more polarized.

Caesar was well-guarded by his 13th Legion, so he crossed the Rubicon River into Rome on January 10, 49 B.C., and he entered the city soon after. A massive Civil War broke out in Rome, and Pompey Magnus fled south, where he was eventually hunted down and killed. As Julius Caesar took control of the city, the Optimates devised a plan to assassinate him on the Senate floor. The assassination, which was an attempt to salvage the Republic, was carried out on March 15, 44 B.C. In the words of Cicero, "All honest men killed Caesar. . . . Some lacked design, some courage, some opportunity: none lacked the will." After the assassination, it enraged the Populares even more, and Rome descended into mob rule. Cicero, being seen as the main advocate for the Republic, was now a public enemy to Rome—he was assassinated on December 7, 43 B.C., his head was formally displayed on the Senate's rostra, his tongue was pierced with pins from Mark Antony's wife Fulvia, and his hands were both cut off and nailed to the Senate doors, according to accounts from Cassius Dio. In the same year, however, the son of Julius Caesar, Octavian Caesar, rose from the ashes and promised to unify the country. He was elected as the youngest Consul in the history of the Republic. Then, formally in 31 B.C., Octavian declared himself as Augustus, took control of Rome, dismantled the Roman Republic, and became the first Emperor of the Roman Empire.

The expectations of civic virtue in the Roman Republic were the combination of Ancient Athens and Sparta. Rome was the largest metropolitan city in the world, up to that point, so their civilization was highly advanced. Their pursuit of scientific enlightenment can be seen through their technological advancement and infrastructure. They devised a series of aqueducts to filter water throughout the city, invented the first surgical tools, created concrete that was used for roads and buildings, mastered advanced weaponry for the military, and created both Roman numerals and a new calendar. The pride of their city, however, was their infrastructure. In John Stambaugh's *Roman City*, it is rumored that they used so much marble in the construction of buildings that, on a sunny day, the people passing by the city would be blinded by the Sun's reflection. Advancements in architecture also led to the creation and implementation of domes and Corinthian columns, which could be seen on most of the buildings in the city.

It is evident, based on the design of their city, that the Romans placed a high value on excellence. Opposite from Aristotle, the Roman definition of excellence can be heard from Marcus Tullius Cicero, who said "Faithfulness and truth are the most sacred excellence and endowments of the human mind." Cicero gives us two important attributes of being a Roman citizen: faithfulness, according to Kathryn Tempest's *Cicero: Politics and Persuasion in Ancient Rome*, refers to being faithful both to the state and to one's family, and truth refers to the pursuit of knowledge, which encompasses scientific, agricultural, political, philosophical, and economic knowledge.

With regard to faithfulness, we see a clear similarity to ancient Sparta. Roman citizens, including soldiers, were expected to have an unquestionable loyalty to Rome. One incredibly interesting fact was that military members were not allowed to wear their uniforms within the bounds of the city. The reason for this societal norm was to restrict the possibility of a military coup. Therefore, soldiers would discard their uniforms and put on their white robes prior to entering the gates, which was observed as a sign of loyalty to the Senate, the Consuls, and the entire Republic. In addition, one's public form was the most important form of a person; it was highly criticized to defame or question another citizen's honor or integrity in public, unless there was specific evidence of wrongdoing. In other words, people were criticized in private, but praised in public. Adhering to this simple societal norm helped maintain civility, and contributing to civility gave one even more honor and respect than they previously had. Lastly, faithfulness was not only a standard for men, but also for women. In the Roman Republic, according to Richard Bauman's *Women and Politics in Ancient Rome*, there was a principle of ethics that related to sexual behavior, and it was called *Pudicitia*, which translates to "modesty" or "sexual virtue." Both a woman's appearance and her sexual history were indicators of her morality. Wives were expected to be faithful to their husbands, just as husbands were expected be faithful to their wives, and any deviation from this course of action would destroy the individual's personal reputation. To summarize, one of the main virtues of excellence in Rome was faithfulness, which correlates to being faithful to the state, to others, and to one's spouse.

The other Roman virtue that Cicero spoke of is truth. Truth refers to, in the Platonist sense, the pursuit of knowledge for one's self, one's community, and one's country. In Rome, citizens derived pleasure from learning, which is illustrated through the society's technological advancements, innovations, and discoveries. Most of the rhetoric surrounding scientific knowledge in the ancient world refers to Greece, but Rome also made groundbreaking discoveries. Varro helped revolutionize the field of agricultural management with *Res Rusticae*, Lucretius continued research on optics and biology by writing *De Rerum Natura*, Nigidius advanced the concepts of astronomy and weather, and Vitruvius applied mathematical theories to architecture to create schematics for new buildings in *De Architectura*. The Roman populace was driven by scientific enlightenment and discovery, but Cicero's "truth" also refers to honesty. The only exception to attacking someone's personal reputation publicly was if you had evidence that the other individual participated in wrongdoing, which set the basis for the Roman legal system.

The law in Rome was considered more important than the people were because it connected the entire society together better than any special interest group could. The first codified form of law in Rome, which was created in 451 B.C., was known as the Twelve Tables. Contrary to Sparta or Athens, Roman Law applied to all citizens, even to the leaders in the Senate, according to Andrew Riggsby's *Roman Law and the Legal World of the Romans*. Everyone was held accountable under the Roman Republic. The military of Rome used a separate code of conduct, but they were still bound by the Twelve Tables whenever they were present in the city or amongst another major population center. The most interesting advancement in Roman Law was that the protections, and privileges, granted under law only applied to Roman citizens. Rome, early in the Republic's history, had a vastly inclusive immigration system, but the Republic never granted full citizenship rights to non-citizens, due to fears spread amongst the Patricians that doing so would be the downfall of the city.

What we see from our case study of the Roman Republic is that the same principles seen in both Athens and Sparta were present. The Roman society granted preference to its own citizens over non-citizens, but there were specific expectations for Roman citizens that everyone had to adhere to. The civic virtue of Rome was first centered around faithfulness, meaning every citizen shared a unified, common loyalty to the state of Rome, and every citizen acted in public with honor. Fidelity was expected from both men and women of the city, as each citizen acted with faithfulness towards their neighbors, fellow citizens, and spouses. The Roman society was also predicated on truth, which meant citizens actively pursued knowledge and discovery in all facets of life. Romans were constantly analyzing how systems could be improved, from an economic, social, political, and military perspective. There was also heavy emphasis on science and mathematics, which is demonstrated through the Romans' advancements in astronomy, engineering, and architecture.

The Ancient worlds of Greece and Rome were, to the Founders and Framers of the U.S., the pinnacles of human civilization. These societies would become instrumental in the construction of America's political beliefs and ideologies, economic policies and directives, and ethical and moral philosophies. The Founders saw the U.S. as a continuation of these great Ancient societies, which will now be explored.

NOTES

1. History.com Editors, "Ancient Greek Democracy," p. 1
2. Standford.edu, "Democracy," sec. 2.3
3. John Adams, "From John Adams to John Taylor, 17 December 1814"

4. James Madison, *Federalist No. 10*
5. Daniel Wegner, "Paradoxical Effects of Thought Suppression"
6. Christopher Harress, "Why do so many in Alabama oppose same-sex marriage?"
7. Lisa Wade (*Business Insider*), "Why southern states are the leading consumers of gay porn"
8. Michele Meleen, "What do kids think about school uniforms?" sec. 3
9. Scholastic, "School Uniforms—Survey Results"
10. Thucydides, *The Peloponnesian War*, p. 82
11. PSU.edu, "The Struggle of the Orders"
12. BBC, "Julius Caesar"

Chapter 2

The Foundations of American Citizenship

The purpose of this chapter is to illustrate the civic virtues that were present at the founding of the United States of America in 1776. As we will explore, the U.S. was established utilizing the same citizenship expectations as Ancient Greece and Rome. For reference, the Founders of the U.S. refer to the members of the Second Continental Congress, who signed the Declaration of Independence in 1776, and the Framers of the U.S. refer to the delegates of the original thirteen states who wrote, debated, and voted to ratify the Constitution at the Federal Convention of 1787. There are inherent civic virtues that are both expressed and implied from our two founding documents: the Declaration of Independence and the U.S. Constitution. First, we will analyze, briefly, how the U.S. came into being.

THE HISTORY OF THE COLONIES

The major world superpowers in the west, at the cusp of the sixteenth century, were Great Britain, France, and Spain. According to Alan Taylor's *American Colonies: The Settling of North America*, these European powers were in the business of establishing Empires, which meant territorial expansion for the sake of economic prosperity. While France colonized the northern territories in modern-day Canada, Spain worked south towards modern-day Florida, Louisiana, and Mexico. Their movements for expansion led to the middle of modern-day America being vacant, so the British seized the opportunity. The first permanent English colony was in Jamestown, Virginia in 1607. The early English colonies in America were able to capitalize on the rich, fertile soil of the New World, which led to the creation of agricultural hubs. Specifically, the Jamestown colony was able to thrive due to the cultivation of tobacco. Other English colonies began to sprout throughout the modern-day northeast region, and there is a massive misconception about these colonies. The common narrative is that the Pilgrims arrived in 1620 to escape religious persecution from the Church of England. While this is true to a point, the Puritans never intended to establish a new society here based on religious freedom—rather, their goal was to create a religious utopia. Any member of the society who deviated from their beliefs was ousted. The only societies in the New World who supported true religious freedom were those dominated by the Quakers, which primarily resided in modern-day Pennsylvania.

The creation of geographic, unified theocracies became the norm in colonial America. However, once major centers of commerce were established in the northeast, the British government increased its political influence, which led to a surge in immigration according to Newton Mereness's *Travels in the American Colonies*. American colonies then became known for diversity in the eighteenth century, with colonies in South Carolina being economically, religiously, and politically different from the colonies of Connecticut. The geographic separation of America across the Atlantic Ocean from Great Britain created a sensation of autonomy throughout all of the colonies. In the 1700s, Britain increased their political and economic dominance through the passage of laws in their Parliament, and the colonists had no representation. The events that led to the American Revolution are too numerous and complex to be cited in this work, as we are only concerned about the expectations of civic virtue that were present at the creation of the United States. In summary, however, according to Edward Gray's *The Oxford Handbook of the American Revolution*, the war was sparked by Britain's restrictions of political, economic, and social liberties. In response to the lack of freedom, the Founders met in Philadelphia, modern-day Independence Hall, and convened the Second Continental Congress on May 10, 1775. At this point, the Revolution had already begun, but the delegates wished to create a formal declaration of their split from Great Britain. In *American Scripture: Making the Declaration of Independence*, Pauline Maier wrote that the document was primarily authored by Thomas Jefferson, but Benjamin Franklin and John Adams both had input in the final document. It was signed by the presiding officer of the Congress, John Hancock, on July 4, 1776. The other Founders were scattered throughout the United States, but they made their way to Philadelphia to sign the document over the course of the summer in 1776. When every signature was solidified, the country sent the declaration to King George in England.

THE DECLARATION OF INDEPENDENCE

While the Declaration did not establish any specific form of government, it did lay out the basic principles and philosophies of the new nation, and it listed specific reasons why the U.S. decided to become a series of free and independent states. The principles within the Declaration were revolutionary for their time, much like Athenian democracy in the ancient world. As a disclaimer, the U.S. in 1776 was far from perfect—there were economic disparities, such as income inequality, political disparities, such as an informal class system which benefited white males over all other groups, and social disparities, such as the evil of slavery. This work is, in no way, arguing that the early government of the U.S. was great, but rather we are arguing that the *idea of America* was great. It was a collection of perfect principles, which were implemented to civil society by imperfect men. Nevertheless, the revolutionary ideals from within the Declaration have had more of a positive impact on the modern world than any other document in human history.

At the core of the document, Thomas Jefferson lists three distinct lines that separated America from every other civilization of the time. While these three ideas were not actually unique, the combination of all of them, in the same society, was revolutionary. The ideals central to the new U.S. were 1) all people are born equal under God, 2) government should reflect the will of the people, and 3) all citizens have an inherent honor that is of the divine nature. We will examine each of these principles separately, along with their ramification for civic virtue.

The first ideal illustrated by the Declaration of Independence is that all citizens are born equal. Jefferson writes that, "We hold these truths to be self-evident, that all men are created equal, that they are endowed by their Creator with certain unalienable Rights, that among these are Life, Liberty and the pursuit of Happiness." We discussed earlier the Roman definition of truth, as implied by Cicero's *De finibus bonorum et malorum*. At the heart of America is also truth, but in the U.S., it is envisioned that truth represents the idea that all people are created, or born, equal under God. At birth, every human has inherent value, and they are entitled to life, liberty, and the pursuit of happiness. This iconic line from Jefferson derives from John Locke's Second Treatise on Civil Government, where he states that all men have the right to "life, liberty, and property." From this concept, we can infer three separate civic virtues: adherence and obedience to law, personal responsibility, and a duty to strive for excellence.

By stating that all people have a right to life, Jefferson is suggesting that citizens subsequently have a responsibility to adhere to, and obey, the law. If one person deprives another of life, then he or she should have to forfeit their own. Life is amongst the most precious of gifts as a human being, so it should be protected at all costs. Jefferson, by writing about the right to life, lays the foundation for the American criminal justice system. By stating that all people have a right to liberty implies that citizens should be responsible, and be held accountable, for their own decisions. Once again, the expectation of personal responsibility hints at the criminal justice system. The U.S. was founded on the ability of an individual to act freely, as long as his actions do not interfere with the freedoms of others—an important concept which will be revitalized by James Madison in the drafting of the Bill of Rights. Lastly, Jefferson argues that all people have a right to the pursuit of happiness. He does not explicitly exclaim, nor infer, that all people have a right to happiness, but rather that they should have the right to pursue it, meaning all people have a responsibility to themselves to strive for excellence. Recall, earlier in this work I referenced a letter from Jefferson to William Short in 1819, in which Jefferson identifies himself as a philosophical Epicurean. The Epicureans were seekers of pleasure, but they believed that knowledge and intelligence were the keys to obtaining pleasure—one does not gain eternal, long-lasting happiness through physical or sexual acts, but through the pursuit of knowledge. Jefferson used the Declaration of Independence to ingrain the idea of pursuing knowledge into the culture and populace of the United States, which was the cornerstone of ancient Athens. All people have a responsibility to pursue knowledge for the betterment of all mankind, which will lead to happiness in the soul.

The second revolutionary ideal seen in the Declaration of Independence is that government should reflect the will of the people. Jefferson continues by referencing the aforementioned rights, stating "That to secure these rights, Governments are instituted among Men, deriving their just powers from the consent of the governed." Therefore, the government should be a direct reflection of the people. However, this concept goes both ways, which was a fear shared by John Adams. If the people are intelligent, physically fit, and ethical in both thought and action, it will culminate in a ruling class that reflects those values. Conversely, if a population is opposite of these traits, it will inspire unintelligent, lazy, corrupt political actors, which will threaten the longevity of the country. The Founders were all well-read on the tragedy of ancient Athens, so they included this line as a warning to the citizens not to become comfortable with mediocrity, since they are the ones who naturally manifest the government. Jefferson, therefore, believes it is essential for the populace to strive for excellence in all facets, thereby ensuring the stability and integrity of the U.S. government.

Lastly, Jefferson argues that all people have honor. He concluded the Declaration of Independence with, "And for the support of this Declaration, with a firm reliance on the protection of divine Providence, we mutually pledge to each other our Lives, our Fortunes and our sacred Honor." At the time of the founding, the honor of individuals referenced their ethics and morality, according to Richard Beeman's *Our Lives, Our Fortunes, and Our Sacred Honor: The Forging of American Independence, 1774–1776*. Most interestingly, Jefferson places the word "sacred" in front of honor, meaning that honor is inherently divine.

The predominant religion at the time was Christianity. According to David Holmes's *The Faiths of the Founding Fathers*, the Founders were all predominantly Christian. In the Bible, there is a story of Peter in which his conviction for Christ led to his crucifixion by the Roman Empire. The central idea in these lines, which Jefferson puts on full display, is that it is better to suffer and die, while defending one's morals and beliefs, than to live as a coward with a malleable belief system. All of the Founders, if captured by the British government, would have been executed—Benjamin Franklin, at the Second Continental Congress, addressed dissent from his fellow Pennsylvanian John Dickinson by stating "We must, indeed, all hang together or, most assuredly, we shall all hang separately." The Founders, including Jefferson, were all well-aware of the risk to what they were doing, but they still proceeded to venture into the darkness of posterity for their convictions.

Defending one's beliefs has roots in both ancient Greece and Rome. Specifically, the value of maintaining one's convictions can be seen clearly by analyzing the fall of Melos during the Peloponnesian War. Athens planned to gain control of the island to use it as a strategic stronghold against Sparta. When the Athenians arrived at the island of Melos, the Melians had two options: fight, or surrender. Fighting would surely result in them being killed, since the Athens army was far superior, but surrendering would mean that they would have to assimilate to the Athenian culture, which included adjusting their religious practices, ethics, governmental structure, and economic policy. The Melians chose to fight, knowing they would all perish. From an excerpt from *The Peloponnesian War*, Thucydides highlights what is known as "The Melian Dialogue." In the end, the Athenians "put to death all the grown men whom they took, and sold the women and children for slaves, and subsequently sent out five hundred colonists and inhabited the place themselves." The lesson from the Melians was shared by the Spartans, as previously discussed by analyzing the Battle of Thermopylae. To the Founders of the U.S., defending one's beliefs, even in the face of danger, was the greatest honor they hoped to instill in the populace, and it was quite sacred.

THE U.S. CONSTITUTION

We have examined the Declaration of Independence in detail and have extracted the expected civic virtues and standards of excellence from the Founders. After the U.S. won the Revolutionary War, with the help of France, they instituted the Articles of Confederation. However, these articles proved insufficient for cultivating a unified, strong nation due to the weakness and limited powers of the national government. In response, the Framers met in Philadelphia to revise the governmental structure of the country. The Federal, or Constitutional, Convention led to the creation of the modern-day U.S. government. We will next analyze the Constitution, paying close attention to specific formations of structures which were intended to protect and defend the liberty of citizens. The government, as will be explored, is the culmination of Athens, Sparta, and the Roman Republic.

SEPARATION OF POWERS

Separation of powers is a concept that helps create a horizontal conflict amongst the branches of the national government—if the federal level is always fighting amongst each other, as the theory goes, it will not have the time or resources to strip liberties from the people. The legislative branch, called the Congress, is responsible for making all laws, with additional responsibilities including declaring war, levying taxes, passing a budget, and regulating interstate commerce. It is the primary branch, which is evident from the fact that it was placed in Article I. The legislature is made up of two chambers: the House of Representatives (lower house), and the Senate (upper house).[1] The House is elected directly by the people located within each of the Congressional districts, and members serve two-year terms. The Senators were originally appointed by the State legislatures, but now they are also directly elected; they serve six-year terms, and only 1/3 of the chamber is up for re-election every two years. The benefit of the bicameral legislature is that it is unlikely to be heavily influenced by the immediate passions of the people; that is, the process of passing laws will take longer. The lower house is where all the debate will take place; Congressmen will fight viciously in the House to enact their ideas. Oppositely, the Senate is the "cooling chamber" where the passions will settle down and responsible decisions can be made. After a bill is passed through both houses, it is sent to the President to be signed into law.

The legislative branch is a combination of the political theory of Rome. Rather than letting every citizen vote on matters directly, they elect representatives to vote on their behalf. Whereas Rome was a single body controlled by two individuals, the Senate led by two Consuls, the Framers established a bicameral legislature, with one leader in each chamber. This way, the minority party will not be crushed by the majority, which protects against the Capitol becoming a partisan war zone where every term consists of the majority party simply undoing what the previous majority had done. The construction of the legislature, as it is laid out by Article I, is slightly unique because it ensures that the majority of the country's power is held directly accountable from the populace.

The next branch, the Executive branch, is charged with enforcing the law. The head of this branch is the President, whose name derives from "Presiding Officer."[2] He is elected indirectly—there are a series of Electors in each State, and during every election the people vote for who they believe the Electors should vote for. So, the people do not actually elect the President of the United States—this system is called the Electoral College. Second in command is the Vice President, who presides over the Senate, and is authorized to break any ties in that chamber. The executive has control over the military, which is specified as the "Army and Navy." Overall, the President has the power to control the military, appoint foreign ambassadors (with approval from the Senate), nominate court members (with confirmation from the Senate), grant pardons, and veto bills passed through the legislative branch—however, this veto can be overridden with 2/3 majority in each chamber of Congress. The executive is also given implied emergency powers through the "Take Care" Clause to deal with any national crisis. The origin of this clause can be traced back to Sparta, where one leader would become a dictator during times of crisis—an effective system because in times of war, decisions must be made quickly and without heavy deliberation and debate. Over the past century, there is no doubt that the Executive branch has become more powerful, but at the early stages of the country it was well-restricted.

The Judicial branch is the third, and final, branch in the U.S. government. It is comprised of the court system, with the highest being named the Supreme Court.[3] It does not specify how many Justices need to be on the Supreme Court, but initially there were six. Today, that number has expanded to nine. This is often regarded a "separate but not equal" branch because it has neither the power of the purse nor the sword. The court may only decide "cases and controversies" between two parties—they do not have the power to declare a newly passed law unconstitutional by their own accord. All federal judges are nominated by the President and confirmed by the Senate; they serve life sentences because the Framers did not want them to be swayed by the political pressures of the populace. In lower courts, as well as state courts, the Constitution guarantees defendants the right to a trial by jury. This principle, which allows for private citizens to act as jurors, was taken directly from ancient Athens. It ensures an equal judicial platform predicated on due process and fairness.

CHECKS AND BALANCES

We call this system of three overlapping branches a conflict because each branch has specific powers over the other—a system called checks and balances. For example, the Congress may deny the nomination of a Justice or Ambassador, override a Presidential veto, and impeach the members of the other two branches. The President can veto legislative bills, and he is the one who nominates federal court members. The judicial branch can declare laws and acts unconstitutional (assuming the laws and acts arise from a case or controversy), and the Chief Justice of the Supreme Court is the one who presides over the impeachment trial of the President—the House of Representatives can pass impeachment articles, but only the Senate can charge the President and remove him from office. The powers each branch has over one another work to prevent any one branch from becoming too powerful, and thus oppressive to the country and its people. Checks and balances help to create fierce division between these branches, but that is by design, just as the separation of powers was—it helps preserve individual liberties.

FEDERALISM

The next conflict is a vertical conflict, and it can be summarized by the word federalism. Madison, just as he stole the idea of separation of powers from both the Roman Republic and from French philosopher Baron de Montesquieu, also stole the idea of federalism. The first traces of the distribution of powers amongst different levels of government comes, surprisingly, from the Native Americans—a spoken system of law called The Great Law of Peace, of the Iroquois Confederacy.[4] The idea was intended to create a conflict between the three different levels of government: the national (or federal) level, the state level, and the local level. The national government has the power to do anything the Constitution grants it the power to do. However, under the Tenth Amendment, any power not specifically granted to the national government shall be reserved "to the States . . . or people." This allows the states to exercise their own digression, and it prevents the national government from becoming tyrannical over the states.

SUMMARY OF ANCIENT INFLUENCES

As has been illustrated, the governmental structure of the U.S. derived from ancient worlds, specifically Athens, Sparta, and the Roman Republic. We can also see that the expectations of civic virtue and standards of excellence in America are the culmination of those once-great societies. However, rather than focusing on one specific society, the Founders and Framers combined all three of them to create nothing short of a magnificent government, operated by virtuous and excellent citizens. Let us reexamine, and summarize, the government structure, civic virtues, and standards of excellence in America and their link to the ancient societies of Greece and Rome.

One citizen of Philadelphia saw Benjamin Franklin departing from the Constitutional Convention in 1789 and decided to ask him what government the Framers had just created, and he responded with "A Republic, if you can keep it."[5] The Founders and Framers, as previously stated, were educated immensely on the history of the ancient world. In fact, leading Founding Fathers such as Thomas Jefferson, James Madison, and John Adams were all fluent in Latin, and they would frequently read about Roman society in that language. The Father of the U.S. Constitution, Madison, knew that democracies always exhaust themselves and commit suicide due to the rise of factions and partisanship. Therefore, he decided to strip some power from the general population, which meant entrusting a handful of educated aristocrats to make policy decisions for the entire nation. The system of representative democracy that is seen through analysis of the Constitution is a Republic.

The major legislative body of the Roman Republic was the Senate, and the Senate is also the upper house of American Congress. The lower house of the U.S. was originally the only legislative chamber that was directly elected by the people, which mirrors the Roman Magistrates. Together, the House of Representatives and the Senate make up the law-making body of the United States, which correlates to the legislative system of the Roman Republic. In addition, in Rome the Senators were granted certain protections in society, and the same goes for members of the U.S. Congress. For example, they cannot be arrested on the way to cast their vote for any reason besides treason or a felony. Roman Senators and American Congresspeople are also linked by their typically high socioeconomic status. The members of our Congress, on average, are far better off financially than the districts and states they represent, and their living standards are, subsequently, well above the average living standards of the country.

The executive authority of the U.S. rests in the President and Vice President. Similarly, in Sparta there were two kings, both being sovereign. The Kings, like the Presidents, were in charge of enforcing the law that the legislative body made, and both Spartan Kings and American Presidents are the commanders of the military. We also see ties between Presidents and the Consuls of Rome. In times of crisis, the U.S., through the War Powers Act of 1973 and the "Take Care" clause of the U.S. Constitution, grants the President almost dictatorial power and authority; in Rome, the Consuls would overrule the Senate in times of crisis and govern as Sovereigns until the crisis was averted. The Executive Branch of the U.S. has roots that can be traced back to Greek and Roman governments.

The blueprint for the Judicial Branch of the U.S. was also stolen by Madison from the ancients. Neither in Sparta, nor Rome, were normal citizens given the ability to decide judicial matters. Both the executive and legislative authorities of their societies had final command of who manned those posts. Similarly, in the U.S. the President nominates Supreme Court Justices and other federal judges, which then depends on the Senate to confirm the nominees. In Athens, every day, common people were selected to serve as jurors. In the U.S., citizens are frequently selected to serve on jury duty, and that action is highly regarded as an expectation of all citizens to ensure each defendant receives an honest and fair trial based on due process.

In addition to government structures, the expectations of civic virtue and standards of excellence from Athens also correlated to the United States. In Athens, their democratic experiment established specific expectations of scientific enlightenment, discovery, and the ultimate pursuit of knowledge. From Plato to Aristotle, Athens expected civic participation and demanded that every citizen pursue excellence at all times. The areas of excellence were commonly noted as philosophical excellence, moral/ethical excellence, governmental/political excellence, and athletic/physical excellence. Citizens were expected to act as one, unified populace with a common direction, act within legal and ethical guidelines, actively participate in government affairs, and strive for physical greatness through being healthy.

During the early days of the United States, the Founders mirrored the same virtues as the Athenians. Many of the Founders actively pursued knowledge and scientific enlightenment. Ben Franklin, for example, made advancement in science in the fields of optics and electricity—he invented the bifocals and was the first to discover the link between electrical charges and lightning. With regard to discovery, Thomas Jefferson was famous for his many inventions, among them the swivel chair. He also helped improve the agricultural practices of his time by separating different forms of crops at his home, Monticello. The Founders all advocated for high citizen participation in the judicial and political process, and they also advocated for higher voter turnouts in elections. Above all, though, the Founders and Framers embodied Athenian excellence. They created a new form of government, helped write the initial form of criminal law in accordance with ethical and religious principles of common decency, revolutionized the theoretical juxtaposition between the citizen and liberty, and helped cultivate one of the most powerful militaries of the eighteenth century with elite warriors.

The expectations of civic virtue and standards of excellence demonstrated by Sparta also contributed to the early days, and formation, of the American polity. Sparta was a timocratic military society centered around honor. To give one's life for the glory of Sparta was the highest honor they could possibly achieve. By Spartan law, soldiers were prohibited from retreating or surrendering, no matter how great the odds. Each individual had honor, making their public form and reputation extremely important, so people defending their honor in battle and against political adversaries. Women also granted an important function in Spartan culture, where their primary roles were to raise children, nurse soldiers back to health, and offer emotional support for their husbands during times of intense training and war.

The subject of societal and military honor was highly important to the Founders. As Jefferson wrote in the Declaration of Independence, honor was considered Sacred, and each person defended their honor in public. In addition, during the Second Continental Congress, the body had to choose a new commanding officer, General, for the Continental Army, and they selected a Colonel by the name of George Washington. Washington's reputation for honor from the war gave him such an elite aurora of glory that they selected him as the first President of the United States. In the early days of the country, citizens would be willing to defend their honor, and their country, to the end.

The basis of civic virtue and excellence in ancient Rome helped create one of the most dominant societies, and long-lasting republics, of all time. As Cicero explained, the main virtues in Rome were faithfulness and truth. Faithfulness referred to two things: first, it referred to the loyalty citizens were supposed to have to their country, and second, it referred to the faithfulness citizens were supposed to have towards their community and spouses. The people of Rome understood that it takes every citizen to make a society work, so they acted with the utmost respect for their peers and for their country. People in Rome always dressed in their best robes so that they would look highly presentable in public. In private life, husbands were highly faithful to their wives, and vice versa. The ideal Roman woman was the symbol of fidelity, perfection, beauty, and strength—women were viewed as divine and angelic. Lastly, Rome cultivated a culture of truth, with everyone pursuing knowledge. They revolutionized agriculture, astronomy, politics, weaponry, and architecture. Everything about the Romans, from the infrastructure, down to their robes, represented the epitome of excellence and knowledge, which was carried over to the early United States.

The standards of virtue in ancient Rome can be clearly illustrated in the early days of the United States. The Americans instituted a new government based on principled and ethical leadership, which was comprised of principled and ethical statesmen. The military was highly respected in society, and they were extraordinarily loyal to their country and its founding principles. There was also widespread collaboration in society, and every citizen frequently debated and deliberated with one another in a free and open society, where there was no fear of retribution for free ideas. The citizens of the U.S. also pursued truth. The very construction of Washington D.C. proves this. The city was centered around the Capitol and was organized in an extremely orderly way. Our buildings were constructed using marble, columns, and domes, which reflected our philosophical roots of Greece and Rome. The capital city's architecture proved to the world that the country was going to be one centered around freedom, reason, and logic. Into the nineteenth century, the U.S. cultivated the world's greatest military, infrastructure, and economic growth through hard work and technological advancements. The U.S. grew from one small colony in Jamestown to a world superpower in less than two hundred years, and it was the first country to successfully combine the concepts of nationalism and free speech, which was only possible through a well-educated and informed citizenry that pursued honor. The greatness of the modern-day United States is owed, in its entirety, to the governments of the ancient world. Without Athens, Sparta, and Rome, there would be no America.

Today, America is still the greatest superpower in the world, with the strongest military and economy. However, at two hundred and forty-five years old, the once shimmering and prosperous beacon of Republican government is beginning to crack, just as the marble of the Roman Republic did. Americans are quickly forgetting, with every passing generation, what it truly means to be American.

To express this idea, quickly think about the current state of its politics. The current condition of the U.S. is far weaker than in previous decades. The political institutions of the U.S. are slowly deviating from the original founding principles of the country, which is resulting in a nation that is destroying itself, just as the Greeks and Romans did. Amongst the peril, look specifically at the three branches of the U.S. federal government, and the problematic areas can be identified.

CONCLUSION

To start, the legislative branch of the U.S. is in steep decline. We have seen two political trends of the Congress since the 1990s, both of which are disastrous. First, the Congresspeople seem to only be versed in politics, law, and economics. Although all of these subjects are noble and necessary to sustain human civilization, there are other important subjects that affect the lives of the country's 330 million citizens. According to the Congressional Research Service, in the 111th Congress, approximately 40% of the members possessed Juris Doctor degrees, and if one factors in economics and politics, that number increased to more than 50%. If half of the Congress is only well-versed in politics, law, and economics, then it is bound to be unable to govern for our diverse, technological society. The world today is data-driven, and the members of Congress are failing to understand the principles of how a digitalized society operates. The result, according to Senator Ben Sasse, is that Congress outsources their own jobs to the bureaucracies. And this has, in fact, happened. The U.S. Legislative Branch is dysfunctional—what they do is they package together 1,000+ page documents, that nobody reads, and the bills delegate their power to the alphabet soup agencies of the country. For example, very few in Congress know anything pertaining to aviation, transportation networks, or globally integrated supply chains. Since Congress is not reasonably intelligent enough to legislate on those issues, they delegate to the Federal Aviation Administration. The FAA actually makes the aviation policy that governs people's lives, not the Congress, and these bureaucrats are completely unelected. The solution for this problem is to restore the original function of the Legislature by electing people from a wide variety of backgrounds, each carrying a different expertise that will help the body govern on any issue that presses the Republic.

The other issue with Congress, which has been going on for three decades, is that there are seldom any instances of compromise. The majority party quibbles with the minority for a long period of time, pushes a bill through to law simply because they can, and then when the parties switch in the next election, the former minority party takes the majority and immediately reverses everything originally done. This process manifests itself for decades, which deteriorates the social fabric of the country—according to John Hibbing's *Congress as a Public Enemy: Public Attitudes Toward American Political Institutions*, the inability of the legislative body to compromise leads to rampant polarization and partisanship in the political institution. Indeed, today in the U.S. there are two results of policy: either a complete stagnation where nothing gets done, or a display of force by the majority party, which gets undone when the country experiences its next power shift. The danger in such a system can be seen through Athens. One of the prime reasons why the city-state descended into chaos, according to Thucydides' *The Peloponnesian War*, was that loyalty to one's party overrode their loyalty to the country. In today's American society, the agenda-driven media persuade the masses that scoring political points are more important than the overall success of the nation. The moment the populace abandons all attempts to compromise and unify, the country is on a dangerous downward trajectory.

Analyzing the Executive Branch is even more horrifying than analyzing the Legislative Branch. The last truly great President, gauging greatness on country unification, was Ronald Reagan. In 1984, Reagan won 49 states in the election, losing only the state of Minnesota. Since then, the country has experienced atrocious and downtrodden leadership at the highest level of the U.S. government. George H.W. Bush did nothing substantial, Bill Clinton performed sexual acts with an intern in the Oval Office, George W. Bush created a deregulated economic landscape that gave rise to an economic recession, and Barack Obama led the country to the lowest eight-year economic growth in decades. However, there is only one trait that all of them have in common besides poor leadership: they all contributed to the expansion of the federal government and the power of the state. The increased dependence on the Chief Executive is slowly destroying the carefully designed system of separation of powers and checks and balances instituted by the Framers. Once the Executive Branch becomes too powerful, it will threaten the civil paradigm, since the Executive office tends to always prioritize safety and security over freedom and liberty.

The Judicial Branch of the U.S., as previously stated, possesses neither the power of the purse nor sword. Theoretically, this branch is the least influenced by the political passions of the populace, so it should be the most stable. However, over the past century, the court has also been slowly deteriorating. In the U.S. Constitution, it makes clear that the job of the Legislature is to make law, and the job of the Judiciary is to interpret the laws that Congress makes. Contrary to that purpose, though, the Supreme Court of the United States has acted in ways that have defiled the sanctity of the entire court system.

In the 10th Amendment to the U.S. Constitution, it makes clear that any power not specifically granted to the national government shall be reserved to the states. The 10th Amendment is often at odds with the 14th Amendment, which houses the "Equal Protections" clause, stating that all citizens must receive equal protection under the law. Take the *Obergefell v. Hodges* case from 2015, for example. This landmark decision nationalized the legalization of gay marriage. Personally, I like many citizens in the U.S. support gay marriage, but this landmark case set a horrible precedent. Under the logic of the 10th Amendment, the federal government had no right to regulate marriage, since it does not list the right to marriage in the Constitution. Therefore, the issue of gay marriage should have been left to the states, to decide individually. In one of the dissenting opinions, Chief Justice John Roberts stated, "If you are among the many Americans—of whatever sexual orientation—who favor expanding same-sex marriage, by all means celebrate today's decision. . . . But do not celebrate the Constitution. It had nothing to do with it." The Supreme Court of the U.S. has issued many opinions since the 1900s, like

Obergefell, that give credence to political passion over Constitutional government. To be fair, though, it is not the fault of the judges. As previously stated, Congress has been delegating its power to agencies and has been stagnate on important social issues. Marriage, which should have been kept in the Legislative Branch as a policy matter, was delegated, in this case, to the court. The Supreme Court, then, acted as an unelected council of nine aristocrats to push a policy decision. The eroding nature of the court mirrors the dissolution of the republican principles of government that make the U.S. unique.

As Thomas Jefferson stated in the Declaration of Independence, the government of the U.S. is based off the "consent of the governed." As John Adams once feared as the second President of the country, that notion carries enormous potential for evil. If the citizenry abandons civic virtue and excellence, it corrodes not only the social fabric and integrity of the country, but also the political institutions which provide stability and order. As polarization, rampant partisanship, and a lack of excellence fired the arrow into the Achilles' heel of Athens and Rome, so it is today in the United States. The problem, thereby, is not with the government, but rather with a U.S. citizenry that has foregone their responsibility to maintain the civic virtues and standards of excellence that the Founders continued from the time of the Greeks and Romans. Being an American means being an honest and honorable knowledge seeker who is loyal to the country, acts with ethics, and strives to achieve physical fitness.

Today, however, the U.S. populace is abandoning these principles, giving rise to shifts in the socioeconomic and political apparatus of the nation. Recall from Athens, when this occurs there are only three possible solutions: the country enters a civil war, it is militarily conquered by an adversary, or it looks to a savior to rise from the ashes and reinstitute the glory of the past. In the case of the U.S., the country took the third option, which will be explored in the following chapter. Without a virtuous and excellent culture of citizenship, the fractured American polity was manipulated into giving power to an absolute demagogue—Donald Trump.

NOTES

1. Uscis.gov, "The Legislative Branch," p. 1
2. The White House, "The Executive Branch"
3. History.com, "Judicial Branch"
4. Terri Hansen, "How the Iroquois Great Law of Peace Shaped U.S. Democracy"
5. Richard R. Beeman, Ph.D., "Perspectives on the Constitution . . ."

*Other sources listed directly in the text.

Chapter 3

Trump Rises from the Ashes of the Elites

In the year 2020, we hear the American left bemoaning the chances of President Trump being re-elected. This claim is especially true; after all, he never should have beaten Hillary Clinton in 2016, if it were not for the nefarious Russians. But what is missed in the Trump Presidency is why he was elected. How could the silent majority exist and why did it overwhelmingly vote for Trump? The ex-urban areas and the second circle suburbs elected him. Is there something wrong with America? I will argue in this chapter that the demise of the American work ethic and insatiable, impulsive greed enabled a candidate like President Trump. In other words, America has become a bastion of lazy, greedy, insatiable people who would likely enjoy electing a boorish, greedy, promising, irrational candidate like Trump. How did America's middle class become so desperate? The easy answer is the failure of the American elites in teaching the right virtues, which include moderation, modesty, hard work, self-reliance, independence, and the shame of living off of the government. Our elites are enabling people into victimhood through the large bloated failing governmental programs of the twentieth century. Now in the twenty-first century the programs are becoming even more generous and more insatiable to resist. Democrats today are proposing free healthcare, free education, free housing, and guaranteed income. Why would any of these programs be needed if the policies of the past were successful? The Democrats acknowledge the failure of the "Great Society" which started fifty years ago by offering reparations for slavery. If the American black community was thriving, possibly the idea of financial reparations would be seen as unnecessary, but since Democrats have failed the black community so overtly, they now intend to bribe the community with the idea of lucrative financial reparations.

We now know that social programs do not lead to prosperity, rather they lead to slothful dependency, which harms the overall nation and its economy.

Economic growth is dependent on consumption and production. Consumption is dependent on individuals having capital and creating capital. Yet, today, we see that most Americans, even after the economic crash of 2008, still only have about $1,000 on average in savings. 75% of Americans live paycheck to paycheck and complain about stagnate wage growth and lack of means to save.[1] So how does any of the socialist ideas of free healthcare and education help the ends of personal prosperity? The simple answer is they do not. Democrats admit the economy is evolving, but into what? I would make the case that the next economy should be one of self-ownership built on personal capital investments to grow and a mature capital without relying on the state or social programs. Maybe the government provides grants to begin personal investing, but the capital must be used to grow capital. Simply put, what return on capital does someone get with free healthcare or free education? Simple answer, none. This point is not to say people want to be dependent on the state, rather the point here is that many people do not have a choice and likely lack the skills and motivation to leave their current communities of poverty. Just quickly, the number of Americans living in poverty today is close to 100 million, making up about 30% of the society. Compared to only 15% in poverty in 1965.[2] Why is the "nanny state" failing? The old socialist governments of the Nordic rim are even abandoning socialism. The Swedish democrats are growing in legitimacy for the first time since the Second World War.

Machiavelli once quipped, "If you set out to deceive the people you will find it is easy to deceive because they are so simple-minded and pre-occupied with their own concerns."[3] How astonishing it is that in America you will hear people on the left complaining that they cannot succeed because of the wealthy. The envy that the lower classes have for the upper class is astonishing. Rather than bemoan one's lower status, why not try harder to learn and acquire the success and wealth of the upper class? President Hoover quipped, "You're not much of a man if you haven't a million dollars by age 40."[4] No doubt, with hard work, determination, and passion Americans can achieve many life goals. But are they striving anymore for such success? Or are they rather waiting for the rise of a socialist state to take care of them? Simply put, a candidate like Trump doesn't happen if America was progressing in the fashion of the American's left, dream for America.

Clearly America is in a state of demise (not necessarily in technological innovation or medical innovation), malaise, and failure all stretching from its dying academic elites and elites in general. Who is the admirable elite that Americans should emulate? You cannot find him or her. This nation is full of dilatants and sycophants trying to gain leverage for personal gain, which means exploiting people either directly through labor or indirectly through sanctimonious holier-than-thou empathy. America has more poor people today than ever before.[5] Something is amiss. An aristocracy must lead, must transform, must mold a society to the virtues that are necessary to sustain it. In constitutional monarchies the monarch embodies and exemplifies the virtues of said monarchy; therefore in republics the aristocracy must embody and exemplify the virtues needed for a mature and healthy republic. Machiavelli thought that the final goal of politics was to educate and to shape their civic conduct. America is void any virtue today. In fact, most people hold the negative action as virtuous, which is dissenting or name calling the President. The wealthy like to keep secret how to make and grow capital because they would rather hoard their cash than teach the rest of us how to make money. This is simply wrong. The aristocracy, just like in the Roman era, should be the "teachers of society." Of course, the academia should reflect the virtues of the aristocracy, which today is far from happening. What virtues are taught in college? Most would likely say tolerance, empathy, and social awareness to inequities in society. How are these virtues applied to make the nation and the individual more prosperous or equipped to succeed in society? Simple answer they do not. Especially since most tolerance warriors are intolerant of an intolerable position. The lack of logic leads to a society easily manipulated and easily duped by demagoguery, from both sides of the political spectrum. The GOP dupes their voters by promising rewards such as tax cuts, open and fair markets, and deficit controls. More often than not, the aristocracy fails to deliver on the promises. Meanwhile the Democrats provide for state sponsored programs which have clearly failed over time, ergo a mad, ignorant, population punishing both parties and disliking Congress and parties at levels never seen before.

In this chapter, I will examine the failure of the aristocracy on issues such as, obesity, victimization, national debt, education, drug dependency, pandering, lack of standards, declining wages, insolvency of social security, loss of economic freedom, and a lack of vision. The elites today just cause noise and trouble in the Republic, in order to rally base supporters in elections. It is as Hobbes said, "The leaders will easily make something that is right, appear wrong and conversely what is wrong look right."[6] In the end the middle class is destroyed setting up the state for a revolution. The rise of Trump is a precursor to America's second revolution. Not just a revolution of words, such as Reagan's revolution, but a revolution of arms and ideas.

The chapter will also examine Plato's thoughts on democracy, Aristotle's idea of "shared excellence," Cicero's on citizenship, and the Founders' ideas on independence. Trump leads the "Populares" and the Democrats, mainly the New England elite are the "optimates." The elites favor the status quo over change, in so doing, the lack of change protects their assets and wealth. For this reason, the elites offer a lot of money in politics to control political leaders and thus dictate "safe" policies.[7]

On the other hand, Trump is seen as a radical populist, declaring himself a nationalist. His main campaign slogan was "Make America Great Again." Just in his campaign slogan alone we have the implied conclusion that America has declined. Who is responsible? I argue the elites are very responsible.

President Trump is certainly an elite, but here I am not interested in explaining the peculiarity of American political ideology, rather in this chapter I make the case that the elites have failed the American people. Trump is not an aberration, rather he is the consequence of the elites failing to teach the masses republican principles. Over the centuries republican principles have mainly evolved from the tradition of resembling the monarchy. Both Cicero and Machiavelli assert the following as main elements of republican principles: civic knowledge, honesty, courage, reverence for the law, popular sovereignty, and reverence for the institutions. From republican principles come civic virtues, which are: being highly informed, honest, courageous, moderate, and having reverence for the law. In the case of the United States, overwhelming citizens have no knowledge of the Constitution; in fact, most surveys indicate a majority Americans cannot identity the Vice President, or any liberty or clauses of the Constitution.

In the current U.S. political environment, the masses are so poorly equipped to defend their liberty that they are losing it. This loss of liberty is especially seen at the airport where Americans must pass through X-rays in order to board an airplane. Why, do we have to do that? The answer is because of the attacks of September 11, 2001, killing over 3,000 innocent Americans. Who is to blame? The U.S. government and the intelligence community. Their failure has led to the creation of the PRISM (data mining and spying program), enhanced interrogations, extraordinary rendition, and numerous foreign entanglements in pursuit of enemy of the state combatants. The failures of the elites and the softening and frankly, dumbing down of the American people, have made the platform of President Trump attractive and reasonable.

Trump and his boorish and often times nasty crass behavior is tolerable to a public that craves more fighting, more chaos, and more division. The elites are crass and boorish. They are incapable of enlightening the masses. This lack of vision is the direct result of a monolithic education in Ivy league institutions. Today's ruling class, from Boston to San Diego, was formed by an educational system that exposed them to the same ideas and gave them remarkably uniform guidance, as well as tastes and habits. These amount to a social canon of judgments about good and evil, complete with secular sacred history, sins (against minorities and the environment), and saints. Using the right words and avoiding the wrong ones when referring to such matters—speaking the "in" language—serves as a badge of identity. Regardless of what business or profession they are in, their road up included government channels and government money because, as government has grown, its boundary with the rest of American life has become indistinct. Many began their careers in government and leveraged their way into the private sector.

We theorize that the ruling class is akin to Plato's theory explaining the demise of timocracy becoming oligarchy. While the elite should be noble, it is still corruptible-which is the case in the U.S. today. The elites at the Founding of our nation were very noble and not corrupt, but today the opposite.

The health of the American Republic is very bad. The common citizens of the nation have lost any sense of the American founding principles, yet at the same time, have clamored for government to become more giving and more benevolent. If any American knew the founding principles, then they would reject the notion of government takeovers of healthcare and education. The quality of meaningful things in the U.S. Republic have declined dramatically, mainly in the area of education; meanwhile the U.S. is experiencing technological advances that make life more convenient and relaxing. Yet, we doubt any consumer understands how their iPhone works, or how their internet works.

Maybe the clearest evidence of an unhappy American public is the "Wrong Track/Right Track" public poll. Gallup conducts this poll quite frequently. On average the poll indicates 60%, and at times, higher think the nation is headed in the wrong direction.[8] These numbers have been consistent in the Gallup finding since the late 1970s. Either Americans are just generally unhappy, or there is something else happening to cause the unhappiness. We propose the root cause of the American tragedy is the elites' inability to produce creative, dynamic policies that would lead to greater individual prosperity. We suggest happiness is connected to self-financial independence and with the consistent decline of American working wages we can see clearly why people are so unhappy.

THE THINKERS ON REPUBLICANISM

The first admiration of republicanism came from Plato who so much despised democracy and in turn favored a political system whereby elites would serve as the leaders of the polity. Plato was always concerned about the rise of "drones" who would stifle production and craft and lead the polity into economic suffering. Plato felt democracy led to more and more pathetic socialist policies that only made the citizenry increasingly pathetic. After all, what good is a social program other than for making more people poor? That was Plato's logic that leaders would pander to the lower classes to win votes and in the end the result would be a lot of poor people suffering under pathetic social programs and a few wealthy people pandering to said poor people. In his case Plato thought democracy would lead to tyranny. What is important for us here is that Plato did advocate for a government lead by an aristocracy that would wisely rule and wisely shape the people toward excellence, moderation, courage, and craft. Together the polity would prosper.

Aristotle gave greater clarity to republicanism by establishing the doctrine of shared excellence. He made it very clear that a leader could only prosper at his job of leading if and only if the people prosper. How can a ruler rule well if the people are ignorant? It would be like trying to rule a kindergarten class when the kids are out of control. This principle of shared excellence means the masses are a part of the ruling class and must hold the virtues necessary to succeed, that is, self-reliance, courage, moderation, reverence for the law, hard work. They cannot possess envy, laziness, or slothful behaviors. Further he argued under the theory of moderation that the middle class should be large and should rule the policy. Here again he emphasized the importance of cooperation between the two major classes, wealthy class and the middle classes. For this to work the middle class must be well educated on the laws of society and must hold high regard for sustaining the Republic. This means the middle class must know policies that benefit or harm the Republic. Looking at the American middle class they are not knowledgeable of the law and are willing to accept policies from the ruling class that could cause an economic nightmare, for example, Medicare for all.

Cicero argued that the most important role a person has in a Republic is being a good citizen. The citizens are the sole power and responsibility in a Republic. They should possess virtue, courage, moderation, reverence for the law, and temperance. They should strive to better themselves and improve themselves constantly. He would use the metaphor of a sculpture. That at birth we are a ball of clay, over time through education we should sculpt ourselves into mature citizens. Looking at the American middle class we do not see sculpted people, rather Harvard studies show a lot of arrested development in the American middle class. Maturation seemed to miss them. Hence, they are easily in support of policies that will eventually destroy the Republic. In America's case any policy that continues to inflate the debt is bad policy.

Finally, the Founders through their own behavior informed us what would make a good citizen. George Washington always presented his best self in public. He wore his best clothes, and embodied the principles of moderation, temperance, compromise, and cooperation. Similarly did Jefferson, Adams, Wilson, and in fact all of them. They all believed that being a citizen in a Republic was a big deal, it meant something. The people are in charge, the people have power, and those who represent them do so as humble stewards, so say the Founders. Of course, today America's ruling class is so corrupt and misguided that Americans do not learn from them, and most likely do not respect them. This is causing the demise of the Republic. The vanity of the ruling class to hold power over the key Republican principles is dragging the nation closer and closer to its demise. The public needs virtues like moderation, courage, tolerance, self-reliance, and civic knowledge; yet we know all of those virtues are in short supply in the modern American Republic. People clamor for handouts from the government. They insist they are victims of a corrupt society. They claim only the rich can get rich. They claim the stock market is fixed for the wealthy. They claim that even if they work hard they cannot get ahead. Frankly, listening to civilian bemoaning over current affairs and status is tiring. People should have examples to look to and set their sights on achieving goals and aspirations. But today in America there are few virtuous leaders, if any at all. Americans feel lost, helpless, and frustrated. In fact I would call it a giant malaise of a spoiled public that wants more from government in exchange for votes. This dependency on government is the great mistake of many nations and civilizations, and likely will do the same to America. America's aristocracy has failed to encourage the right virtues; instead they encourage dependency, slothfulness, carelessness, and envy. Candidates like Trump will no longer be aberrations, rather they will become the mainstay.

Republicanism demands and implores a virtuous society. Capitalism run amok will destroy the middle class. Likewise, the middle class not having any virtues will support socialist candidates who will in turn destroy the Republic and capitalism. A person's best chance for prosperity is through hard work and self-ownership, which includes home ownership, stock investing, and other forms of income derivation. We must teach our people to succeed, not to wait for government to provide some social program. You can throw money at a problem all day and not fix it. In the following I make the arguments which can convince anyone that the data presented clearly shows how the American aristocracy has failed the American people. Just think about this, who is rich in America and who is living a life of luxury-the aristocracy is, and who isn't, the middle class. Who has power, the aristocracy, who doesn't, the middle class. Who is responsible for the future of the Republic, the aristocracy, not the middle class. America needs a virtuous and responsible aristocracy to lead it, nurture it, mature it, and to inspire society. Today, our aristocracy is missing, and we need a new ruling class.

AMERICA AND OBESITY

First, let's look at how the average American is doing at taking care of themselves. I recall on my trips to Europe and speaking with foreign friends that most would describe Americans as blue jean wearing, lazy, and fat. Are Americans fat? The answer is yes.

If we look at child obesity, we see according to the data that since the 1960s the obesity rate in children has gone up fourfold. If we look at the adult obesity rate it ranges from 20% to 35% of adults. Americans are getting fatter over time. Why should we care? Obesity in the United States is a major health issue, resulting in numerous diseases, specifically increased risk of certain types of cancer, coronary artery disease, type 2 diabetes, stroke, as well as significant increase in early mortality and economic costs. While many industrialized countries have experienced similar increases, obesity rates in the United States are the highest in the world.

An obese person in America incurs an average of $1,429 more in medical expenses annually. Approximately $147 billion is spent in added medical expenses per year within the United States. This number was suspected to increase approximately $1.24 billion per year until the year 2030.

The United States had the highest rate of obesity within the G-7 nations. With about 23% obesity in 1962, estimates have steadily increased. The following statistics comprise adults age 20 and over. The overweight percentages for the overall U.S. population are high, reaching 39.4% in 1997, 44.5% in 2004, 56.6% in 2007, and 63.8% (adults) and 17% (children) in 2008.

In 2010, the Centers for Disease Control and Prevention (CDC) reported higher numbers once more, counting 65.7% of American adults as overweight, and 17% of American children, and according to the CDC, 63% of teenage girls become overweight by age 11. In 2013 the Organization for Economic Co-operation and Development (OECD) found that 57.6% of American citizens were overweight or obese. The organization estimates that three-fourths of the American population will likely be overweight or obese by 2020. Figures from the CDC in 2014 found that more than one-third (36.5%) of U.S. adults age 20 and older and 17% of children and adolescents aged 2–19 years were obese. A second study from the National Center for Health Statistics at the CDC show that 39.6% of U.S. adults age 20 and older were obese as of 2015–2016 (37.9% for men and 41.1% for women).[9]

Obesity has been cited as a contributing factor to approximately 100,000–400,000 deaths in the United States per year and has increased healthcare use and expenditures, costing society an estimated $117 billion in direct (preventive, diagnostic, and treatment services related to weight) and indirect (absenteeism, loss of future earnings due to premature death) costs. This exceeds healthcare costs associated with smoking and accounts for 6% to 12% of national healthcare expenditures in the United States.

Nothing good comes from America becoming fatter. The health costs will continue to rise and the need for assistance will only rise. Who is to blame for the rising obesity? Clearly the elites. When was the last time you heard anyone critically talk about obesity in America? Diets are necessary. Obesity is a national crisis. Yet, not a peep out of DC. Rather, the elites provide substance to the increasing obesity, by adopting claims of victimhood. For example, say weight gain is genetic, or a function of a damaged thyroid. Of course the Affordable Care Act took a crack at the obesity rate, but to do so would have to establish government oversight into personal caloric intake—very intrusive. Rather, I argue the elites should make the case that obesity is unacceptable, it is harming the nation, and people should personally work harder to cut back their caloric intake. If America has the right attitude about weight, then obesity would not be an issue. Just take a look at a nation like Japan where they have the right attitude about obesity. It is dishonorable in Japan and China to be fat. Hence, much lower BMI and unhealthy eating in each nation respectively. America can do better, but a lot of its solution is personal, not governmental.

AMERICA'S NATIONAL DEBT

Thomas Paine wrote in *Common Sense* that a national debt, if produced by a common need, that is, a Navy, is a national bond. Well, in America today we are all really bonded together by a massive 21-trillion-dollar national debt. By citizen it works out to 43,000 per household to pay it off.

Data indicates American national or public debt as a percent of GDP. Today debt is about 105% of GDP, up dramatically from its low in the 1980s as 30% of national debt. So what, is what most people would say in light of such data. Three countries have gone bankrupt in recent years: Greece, Iceland, and Portugal. In each case the debt to GDP exceeded 150%. So, possibly the U.S. faces an existential crisis if the debt passes 150% of GDP. We simply do not know. However, President Obama stated years back that the nation's debt is immoral and is a serious problem in the medium time. In fact, on the campaign trail in 2008 he railed against Bush 43's debt spending and taking the war "off the books." Every candidate running for office makes the case that the debt will be a crushing burden on the next generation, yet the aristocracy seems more concerned in having the status quo allow the debt to worsen.

The most recent projections from the nonpartisan Congressional Budget Office indicate that debt held by the public will rise to 93% of GDP in the next ten years, or the highest since just after the end of World War II. From there, the level is expected to hit 150% by 2049, which is well above what economists consider a sustainable level.

The data presents the acceleration of the total debt beginning in the 1980s. The federal budget didn't exceed 1 trillion dollars until 1996, and now stands at about 3.5 trillion dollars, and at the same time the Federal budget became larger the nation's debt grew even faster. At times over 1 trillion dollars a year. Now remember this debt is going up even in times of economic growth. The debt levels worsen in recessions. The aristocracy knows the debt level is bad but are not willing to make the hard choices to reduce spending.

What is horrible about such a large debt is the interest the government pays on such debt. In fiscal year 2018, the government spent $371 billion on net interest, while the Defense Department budget was $599 billion. Social Security benefits cost $977 billion, Medicare $585 billion, and Medicaid $389 billion, according to the CBO estimates. The debt is closing in on exceeding the Defense spending.

But the CBO said interest outlays' rate of growth in fiscal 2018 was faster than that for the three mandatory federal programs: Social Security (up $43 billion, or 5%); Medicaid (up $14 billion, or 4%); and Medicare (up $16 billion, or 3%). In comparison, net interest on the public debt increased by $62 billion, or 20%.

The data indicates how the interest will grow and consume more and more of the national budget. By 2026, holding the ten year at 3.7% the national debt will exceed 762 billion dollars and be about 13% of the Federal budget. By person, about 23,390 in 2026. Given all the spending you would think the American people would be rather pleased with the Federal government, yet poll after poll shows huge dissatisfaction.

The data indicates on average 57% of Americans think the country is headed in the wrong direction. Over time this data does not change much, ranging from 65% to 55% dissatisfaction.

The data indicates just how disliked the representative branch of government is with an approval rating of just 14%. So, you have 435 members of Congress dividing up 3.5 trillion dollars a year and apparently not doing a very good job at using the money to satisfy the needs of the American people. Now some might blame the continued increase of the nation's debt on federal tax cuts.

The highest the marginal tax rates have been were 91% in 1944. This was done to pay down the debt caused by WWII. One might say such action was responsible. Since the 1940s the tax rates have been declining, from Kennedy's tax cuts to Reagan's tax cuts to Bush and Trump's cuts. The aristocracy doesn't want to pay a lot in taxes. A person making over 500,000 dollars a year could handle a tax rate of 60%. Such a rate would leave them with 200,000 dollars after taxes, compared to a 38% rate which leaves them with 400,000 dollars. Yes, the amount of tax is high, but the tax burden is reasonable. Meanwhile a person making 50,000 dollars pays 25% in tax, leaving them with 38,000 dollars. Much more tax burden in the middle and bottom of the marginal tax system.

This uncontrollable spending and debt bearing is strong evidence of a populous that is ignorant on economics. Therefore, they will believe and support the spending promises of unqualified candidates. Madison warned in Federalist No. 51 that "there will be days of madness and foolishness towards printing money or the wicked policies of socialism." The national legislature is supposed to be a revered institution that forms public opinion and educates the masses on democratic policies; rather the legislature is despised. Rousseau said, "the moment you no longer want to see the legislature in action your nation is no longer a Republic." We are clearly at that stage. How does economic ignorance and failed institutions enable Trump? The ignorance is key. Trump preys on ignorant voters. Without doubt, the American voter is ignorant to the demise of the Republic because of the bloated debt. When the markets crash because of the debt obligations and services stop then voters will finally realize how the Aristocrats failed them.

AMERICAN EDUCATION

American education is always a hot debatable topic. Most Americans have strong opinions over the state of public education and the role the government should or should not play in schooling the nation's children. Two recent programs that highlight the debate were President GW Bush's, "No Child Left Behind Act," whereby standardized testing became prominent from third through twelfth grade to ensure students were not getting left behind. This policy ended up being hated by most state educators—they clamored it was too much testing. President Obama replaced the act with "Race to the Top," which some liked and others didn't because again it was test centric. Also, during this time period "Common Core" came out which mandated from state to state the same common core curriculum to ensure standards. Today, states have gone back to establishing their own independent standards but are still in favor of standardized testing to ensure knowledge base standards per child.

What is odd about American education is how test centric and rigid it has become. Children are often learning in styles similar to the 1950s and there is little creativity in the classroom. Alan Bloom reminds us in his famous book *Closing of the American Mind* that moral relativism has destroyed the young person's intellectual curiosity. I certainly agree to this point. You will commonly hear students complain that "The teacher is just teaching to the test," or "What is the point of reading this old document?" or "There are no truths," or "How does this material matter?" What has truly happened in American education is that the student opinion has taken over the classroom. The teacher is no longer the authority; rather the student has become so. Again, if we think of Aristotle's shared excellence theory a teacher can only teach well if their students are well. But, in America, as is true through Western Europe, the youth are insatiable, impulsive, and not curious at all intellectually.

Further, the U.S. does not perform well against international equals. As for the education system, the U.S. is very good. U.S. children, on average, go to well-equipped schools. But this varies from state to state based on funding. But let's talk about quality of education.

The data indicates that the U.S. on a standardized math test scores below the mean of 500. Countries such as China, Germany, and South Korea score about the mean.

The data indicates the U.S. again is behind other competitors. The U.S. scores below the mean on the PISA science test of 500, while countries such as Canada, China, Australia, Japan, South Korea, and Germany score above the mean.

Further, education in the U.S. is vulnerable to mass shootings and an influx of illegal immigrants who hold a foreign language. All of this complicates the school day. But, the point here is that the U.S. education system is lacking when it comes to civic knowledge.

The data gives us some indication of a modest lack of public knowledge. The youth are much more likely not to know current events and leaders. Lack of knowledge can lead to a major change in a nation if the youth are either open minded by a strong intellect or by ignorance. The latter is more likely causing the striking finding of American children favoring socialism over capitalism.

The data indicates that four out of ten Americans now think socialism is a good thing, compared to just 25% in 1942.

What we have to think about dealing with American education is whether or not the education is teaching our children to embrace the ideals, virtues, and innovations of American society and governance. Every child should read Thomas Paine's *Common Sense;* every child should know something meaningful about the Founders and Framers of the nation. Imagine showing Trumbull's famous painting of the Framers signing the Constitution in Independence Hall—what percentage of Americans could identify key figures in the painting? Probably not many. Or let's say they look up in the Rotunda of the Capitol building and see the picture of George Washington. How many would understand the apotheosis of Washington? Cicero warned Caesar not to take the "olive crown" for life and in his letter to Cicero claimed the only way the Senate would do so is because the institution and the society at large had forgotten the virtues of Roman principles. People couldn't name the seven kings, or some of the famous councilors of the Republic. Is the same happening in the U.S.? Our people are losing any sense of heritage, virtue, and meaning in our Republic. This then means we the Republic know morethis is true if we cannot find common cause and common good. Trump certainly was able to prey on the ignorance of voters and was able to spark a "dream" in the minds of some voters by declaring "Make America Great

Again." What did he mean? Is that a "dog whistle"? When was America Great? What determines when America is great? These questions should easily be answered by an informed and participatory public. Yet, I don't think we could get answers easily.

AMERICA'S WAR ON DRUGS

America's War on Drugs started in the 1960s. The goal was to eradicate addiction and death caused by drug use. How well are things in 2019? President Trump asserts massive amounts of drugs pouring into the nation from Mexico. Further, twenty-first century in America is facing an opioid epidemic. How could that happen with the government so pre-occupied with eliminating illicit drug use? In the case of opioids this began by a health industry over-medicating pain pills to patients. The Drug Enforcement Agency, and the Alcohol, Tobacco and Firearms along with border patrol are agencies charged with eliminating illicit drug use, but with little luck.

In 2013, an estimated 24.6 million Americans aged twelve or older—9.4% of the population—had used an illicit drug in the past month. This number is up from 8.3% in 2002. The increase mostly reflects a recent rise in use of marijuana, the most commonly used illicit drug.

Marijuana use has increased since 2007. In 2013, there were 19.8 million current users—about 7.5% of people aged 12 or older—up from 14.5 million (5.8%) in 2007.

Use of most drugs other than marijuana has stabilized over the past decade or has declined. In 2013, 6.5 million Americans aged twelve or older (or 2.5%) had used prescription drugs non-medically in the past month. Prescription drugs include pain relievers, tranquilizers, stimulants, and sedatives. And 1.3 million Americans (0.5%) had used hallucinogens (a category that includes Ecstasy and LSD) in the past month.

Cocaine use has gone down in the last few years. In 2013, the number of current users aged twelve or older was 1.5 million. This number is lower than in 2002 to 2007 (ranging from 2.0 million to 2.4 million). Methamphetamine use was higher in 2013, with 595,000 current users, compared with 353,000 users in 2010.

In the late 1990s, pharmaceutical companies reassured the medical community that patients would not become addicted to prescription opioid pain relievers, and healthcare providers began to prescribe them at greater rates. This subsequently led to widespread diversion and misuse of these medications before it became clear that these medications could indeed be highly addictive. Opioid overdose rates began to increase in the naught decade. In 2017, more than 47,000 Americans died as a result of an opioid overdose, including prescription opioids, heroin, and illicitly manufactured fentanyl, a powerful synthetic opioid. That same year, an estimated 1.7 million people in the United States suffered from substance use disorders related to prescription opioid pain relievers, and 652,000 suffered from a heroin use disorder.[10]

WHAT DO WE KNOW ABOUT THE OPIOID CRISIS?

- Roughly 21% to 29% of patients prescribed opioids for chronic pain misuse them.
- Between 8% and 12% develop an opioid use disorder.
- An estimated 4% to 6% who misuse prescription opioids transition to heroin.
- About 80% of people who use heroin first misused prescription opioids.
- Opioid overdoses increased 30% from July 2016 through September 2017 in 52 areas in 45 states.
- The Midwestern region saw opioid overdoses increase 70% from July 2016 through September 2017.
- Opioid overdoses in large cities increase by 54% in 16 states.[11]

This issue has become a public health crisis with devastating consequences including increases in opioid misuse and related overdoses, as well as the rising incidence of neonatal abstinence syndrome due to opioid use and misuse during pregnancy. The increase in injection drug use has also contributed to the spread of infectious diseases including HIV and hepatitis C. As seen throughout the history of medicine, science can be an important part of the solution in resolving such a public health crisis.

How has the ongoing opioid epidemic and war on drugs, in general, aided President Trump? This further maintains the reality that the aristocracy cannot fix problems. The war on drugs is fifty years old and not near declaring victory.

Quite possibly his most common campaign interest was securing the border, building a wall to keep criminals and drugs out of the country. He even threatened a 5% tariff on Mexican goods to compel them to stem the flow of drugs and illegal immigrants to the U.S. If the aristocracy had actually won the war on drugs Trump would have had much less ammo to use to cause fear and anxiety in the electorate about the ruling-class performance.

Ironically, as America faces a horrible overdose epidemic rooted in opioids and heroine, the government is now pushing to legalize marijuana. How at a time when the nation faces outrageous overdose death totals and addiction totals would the government want to legalize another harmful drug? Of course, the argument today is that marijuana used responsibly is not dangerous; yet it was for decades. Is the aristocracy trying to drug Americans? Make them less stable so they are easier to control? Whatever the answer may be, legalizing marijuana with the high drug dependency rate in this country is complete nonsense and bad policy.

PANDERING TO THE PLEBS

The American elites today find no shame in pandering to win votes. The demagoguery is outlandish in modern American politics. Both political parties gear up the goody bag for every campaign, be it tax cuts, decrease or increase regulations, provide free college, provide free healthcare, free early pre-k, subsidized housing, subsidized food vouchers, fixing the border, infrastructure dreams of high-speed transcontinental rail, and so on. American politics in the modern era does not know the word austerity. Every campaign is about figuring out what the folks want and then promising to deliver it to them. This is no way to lead a nation. The people are important, but they are not absolute in the righteous positions; in fact as we saw with the rising debt, now is the time for America to cut and save, not increase spending.

Of course, in a representative democracy the representatives should represent the people. As Edmund Burke said in a speech to the Bristols, "A Representative has to do what is right for the nation . . . which at times might go against the interest of the citizen." This is true because the representative is more knowledgeable about what is needed and what is not. However, what we see in the U.S. is the persistence of enabling self-dependency on the state while the nation holds a 21-trillion-dollar debt burden. If interest rates were to score about 5%, the nation would lose about 10% of federal receipts to interest on the debt. Simply unacceptable and bad policy.

Machiavelli criticized socialism on the account that "Eventually you run out of your money and have to take from everyone else . . . in this way the once beloved giver is now a cruel miser." Absolutely true, at some point the U.S. will not be able to fund the myriad of social programs. Economic growth cannot and will not last forever. In a recession period the socialist state will be most strained due to its outrageous financial obligations. Take for example the financial crisis in Greece from 2012 to present day. Over 50% of Greek workers worked for the state. The retirement age in Greece was 55 and had some of the most lucrative entitlement programs in the whole Eurozone. The result was a big fat bloated government mounting debt on top of debt. Greek bonds became worthless during the financial crisis and Greece quickly became insolvent by 2012. There, socialism produced drastic misery and austerity. Greece will never be the same economically. Current Greek politics show a move to the right—now realizing socialism is a scam. Edmund Burke quipped, "the rich only become poorer and the poor remain poor" in socialist regimes.

Aristotle quipped as well about the need to own property. Individuals will, Aristotle said, "tend to their own business when they own property . . . happiness is achieved in the form of giving and if you own nothing, then you can never give." Home ownership should be a goal of a person. Self-ownership and financial independence should be a goal of a person. Yet, in America we see a majority of Americans clamoring that the government needs to do more and provide more for the self-interest of the public individual. Why? Senator Graham of Texas once implored Americans are "whiners." Hoover in 1929 thought people would take care of each other and would never want to become dependent on the state. However, over the last seventy years more and more Americans see government as a provider, rather than merely an enforcer. Though socialism has never taken root in the country, the left is clamoring louder and stronger for it in 2019 than ever before. The socialist democrats, known as the "squad," offer juvenile ideas that are unsustainable and frankly un-American. Of course, this is true of any socialist argument. As Lady Thatcher famously quipped, "The problem with socialism is you eventually run out of someone else's money." Just because the U.S. Constitution mentions the word "welfare" in the Preamble does not presume that the Framers advocated for a social welfare state. In fact, we know it was the opposite. Of course, our founders had a few thoughts on pandering and socialism. Thomas Paine wrote, "Beware the greedy hand of government thrusting itself into every corner and crevice of industry." Jefferson in his first inaugural address added, "A wise and frugal government . . . shall restrain men from injuring one another, shall leave them otherwise free to regulate their own pursuits of industry and improvement, and shall not take from the mouth of labor the bread it has earned. This is the sum of good government." President Washington reminds us of the spirit of commerce stating, "A people . . . who are possessed of the spirit of commerce, who see and who will pursue their advantages may achieve almost anything." Adams feared socialism and likened it to the origins of tyranny stating, "The moment the idea is admitted into society that property is not as sacred as the laws of God, and that there is not a force of law and public justice to protect it, anarchy and tyranny commence. If 'Thou shalt not covet' and 'Thou shalt not steal' were not commandments of Heaven, they must be made inviolable precepts in every society before it can be civilized or made free." President Coolidge wisely quipped, "America's business is business." Further, Jefferson knew government would one day become a greedy corporation of politicians serving personal electoral interests, stating, "I wish it were possible to obtain a single amendment to our Constitution. I would be willing to depend on that alone for the reduction of the administration of our government to the genuine principles of its Constitution; I mean an additional article, taking from the federal government the power of borrowing."

In the end American elections are about who will give you more stuff. In a way, politicians are bribing voters for votes. Our political system is nothing more than a transactional democracy. Leaders are bribing voters with incredulous goals, knowing they cannot be accomplished, rather than innovating and proposing New Age policies. This has enabled demagoguery, which is in part why President Trump rose so easily in the Republican field as he pandered goodies to the Republican voter, for example, build the wall, enforce immigration, bring back manufacturing jobs and coal jobs, and so on.

LOSS OF ECONOMIC FREEDOM

The most annoying part of government is not necessarily the laws, certainly not the ones that protect positive freedom; rather it is taxation. The 16th Amendment, probably the worst in American history, enabled the Federal government to impose taxation on income. The Amendment does not specify the means of taxation; therefore, the Feds can tax income any way they want. Taxes are the single most harm to personal freedom in any democratic nation. Taxes drain economic freedom and in America taxation is most cruel. The U.S. uses a marginal income tax rate system. This system withholds taxes prior to an American receiving their paycheck. Think about it, in America, the land of the free, taxes are withheld from the paychecks of almost all Americans. Advocates of the marginal tax rate system claim the system is fair. The easiest way to explain this is that the more money you make the more you are taxed. Currently the system has a three-tier tax rate, 38.5%, 25%, and 15%. Your rate is dependent on your income. Advocates also claim the system is fair because of deductions which allow for a lower taxable income. An important fact is that about 50% of U.S. taxpayers do get their taxes refunded to them each year, but the other half is swamped by the income tax. Now, the Federal government also collects income tax for social security at a rate of 6% and a Medicare tax at the rate of 2.5%. These two taxes are also withheld from the individual's paycheck.

The data indicates that all Americans feel some form of tax burden on their income and yes, the more you make in the U.S. the more you pay in taxes. Some argue that is fair; others say it is not. I would suggest a replacement of the income tax with a national sales tax which then would be a personally owned tax burden based on how much someone is willing to spend. In other words, your tax burden is controlled by your personal consumption: spend more get taxed more, spend less get taxed less; that is fair.

The States and internal municipalities have their own set of taxes. Most states in the Union impose an income tax (only five do not), impose a statewide sales tax, impose property taxes and excise taxes. On average, an American is paying 50% of their income to Federal and State/municipal governments. New York is the worst with an overall individual tax burden of almost 13%. Tax burden indicates the direct and indirect tax responsibility of an individual (combining all taxes). Therefore, the higher the tax burden the less income remains after taxation. As taxes increase, a person's income reduces. As Marx stated, "capital is political power and power in general." If individuals have less money, then it follows they have less freedom and power. Frankly, taxes crush the middle to lower classes the most. As you draw income from the lower classes you reduce the likelihood of social mobility, since after all in a capital system capital is the most important resource. If you are limited in your capital, you are then limited in your mobility. To date, in the U.S., there are very little income incentive programs to enable people to get out of poverty. The idea of a guaranteed income is bantering around, but to date does not exist. I propose offering Americans a large 20,000-dollar tax credit for investment. This money could only be used to invest in the Stock market and would help all Americans in achieving financial freedom, which is real freedom in a capitalist society. Politicians complain that the stock market is not safe for average Americans. This argument is such poppycock. A supermajority of Americans have 401(k) plans, therefore are exposed to the market already. Why not then offer them more direct access? Below is the market movement since 1900.

The data indicates just how much money one can make in the market. The history of the market, even in corrections or crashes, is to move forward and to grow over time. Why aren't most Americans taking advantage of the greatest capital-producing engine in world history? Einstein said the greatest force in the Universe is "compound interest." The answer, elites are steering people away from the market and the formidable financial ignorance of most Americans makes the persuasion of fears, of losing money, the main cause of not investing in the market. But as we see such an argument is nonsense. Just since 2016 the Market composite index value has gone from 18,500 to 27,000. The best social program is a "job," so said President Reagan and with that job Americans should be investing in the market. The Aristocratic incredulous argument of investing is not for the middle class because of loss is a blatant lie. In fact, many of our modern leaders made millions in the market, just ask Speaker Pelosi or Maxine Waters how they made their money and where their money is today; both would say the market. If you want to transform someone's life, education is a small part, the bigger part is capital, and in the U.S. the greatest capital-producing machine ever is the stock market and all Americans should have the ability to invest inside the market, ergo the need for a personal tax credit for investment.

Study participants answered five questions covering aspects of economics and finance encountered in everyday life, such as compound interest, inflation, principles relating to risk and diversification, the relationship between bond prices and interest rates, and the impact that a shorter term can have on total interest payments over the life of a mortgage.

Individuals need at least a fundamental level of financial knowledge. This knowledge, paired with financial decision-making skills, can best ensure an individual's financial capability. Many Americans do not know basic financial questions and have a very limited financial knowledge base. This finding is happening at a time where more Americans than ever are educated and receive federal funds for education. So, this nation is not under-educated, yet it is financially ignorant, how? Why aren't Americans more fluent on the relative factors of economics and personal income strategies? The simple answer, the aristocracy provides very little to no help to the average American for financial knowledge. The aristocracy is keeping knowledge from the American population, under veils of risk or fear. This argument is akin to Marx's argument that capitalists "will modify the means and modes of production whenever necessary," and present capitalism under the "veil of illusions" in politics, religion, and social norms. Is it possible the aristocracy is hiding trade secrets? Yes, and they are doing so to prevent people from rising into the aristocratic class. This is evinced if we look at the American response over the American dream. This is the idea that Americans can make it socially, politically, and financially regardless of the class they are born into. But can they really make it big?

As indicated, many Americans do not believe in the American dream, 31% to be accurate. What is the aristocratic answer to such a finding, is it financial training, or is it a guaranteed income? The latter is the aristocratic answer, which is nonsense. We must implore that government provides financial freedom, not dependency. The American dream is not declining if we taught our people how to make capital, because yes, capital is the main power and force in a capitalist society. All socialism does is promote nationalizing "utility" "in common need" industries for the sake of appeasing the middle classes, it does not to make the middle class wealthier. Take for example Sweden, highest tax rates in the Nordic ring, but what is the per capita income? Sweden ranks 11th in per capita income of about $54,000, while the U.S. ranks 8th with about $62,000, according to the International Monetary Fund as of 2019. Either Sweden has a declining wealthy class, meaning not many millionaires, or the middle class of Sweden is vastly under wealthy compared to the upper class. The latter being the case indicates that in a socialist country you will not achieve wealth equality, such a principle is juvenile and ignorant, nor possible (just ask any Russian during Soviet communism how well wealth equality works). Do we really think more education, and nationalizing industry, is going to transform the middle to lower middle class? No, it will not. What will transform the middle to lower middle class is capital, serious capital. If Americans felt they could go out and make serious money, then they would be moving socially and financially up the proverbial class scale, but today they feel overburdened by taxes, stagnate wages, and hence they are feeling poorer, not richer. Yes, the rich are getting richer in America, but so can the middle class if they had capital and could invest it.

INSOLVENCY OF SOCIAL SECURITY

Social security came about in 1933 during the worst economic depression in American history. The intent of the program was to provide senior citizens a modest guaranteed retirement benefit. The program would work by taxing the worker and paying the retiree. This was a pay in and pay as you go program that when it started had about twenty-five workers for every one retiree. This favorable balance between payee and retiree led to a vast surplus in the program's finances. The government established the Social Security Trust Fund in response to the favorable finances. Unfortunately, the elites in their zealous nature to bribe American voters with transactional ideas, mainly social programs in health and education, began borrowing from the fund. To date, the fund is full of IOUs and is completely zeroed out. Agencies of the federal government owe billions of dollars back to the Social Security Trust Fund.

Today there are about four payees for every one retiree. Slowly the pay in and pay as you go social security program is becoming insolvent. By the year 2035 there will be more retirees than payees, thus making the program insolvent.

The demise of social security is yet another example of how the elites have strangled the American public with insolvency, lack of financial prudence, and creativity in designing a program, and will leave many Americans paying more taxes in order to receive the guaranteed retirement benefit.

CONCLUSION

In this chapter I set out to evince factors showing the perpetual decline of standards and quality of life in the United States. I used the data to argue that the aristocracy is failing the American people. The United States of America cherishes freedom, but as Plato wrote, "freedom is dangerous if not controlled by intellect and reason." In the U.S. we can see how unbridled freedom is consuming the mores of the souls of Americans. They are vastly overweight, either vastly ignorant, or vastly addicted to a pleasure box. America has not evolved into the "shining hill" Reagan called for in the 1980s. Education in America has become a muted down version of indoctrination, not enlightenment. As Alan Bloom warned in 1986 with the "Closing of the American Mind," each generation is more narcissistic and less enlightened. Americans are free but choose unwisely how to use it. The greatest example of the mediocrity of the American people is the emergence of socialist democrat candidates Sen. Sanders and Sen. Warren. Both of them fall over each other trying to come up with more freebies and goodies for the American people. They call their policies "rights," such as healthcare, education, housing, and embrace naked socialism. Socialism is the most juvenile political form. It is not a progressive idea, rather an old idea. It is not transformative, and it is not constitutional. So, why then does anyone listen to them? The answer is easy. The American people are so far from knowing the Constitution and so victimized by their own personal failures and the failure of the elites to enlighten them that they are creating their own doom. The debates in the U.S. have become self-aggrandizing, victimizing baloney. Senator Sanders has achieved little to nothing, as a senator, and is not capable of success in the highest office; yet people clamor for him. The rise of Trump and the counter-revolution of socialism versus capitalism is all the result of the failures of the elites. Clearly, they wouldn't wish for the results they are seeing, but their failure to mature and progress the American people has created a victimized, obese, low educated, intolerant society and people.

NOTES

1. U.S. Census Financial data 2017
2. Ibid., i
3. Machiavelli, *The Prince*, Chapter 10 (Oxford University Press)
4. Hoover, Herbert. *Hoover Presidency*, Donald Theismann, 1945 (Penguin Press)
5. U.S. Census 2018, total was approximately 50 million people, or 25% of working adults
6. Hobbes, Thomas. *The Leviathan*, Chapter 18 (Oxford University Press)
7. 2016 Presidential Election Hillary Clinton raised over $1 billion, business PACS and Super Pacs contributed, in total, over $300 million (Federal Election Commission)
8. Gallup Poll, Wrong/Right Track 1975–2018
9. Gathered from the Center of Disease Control, USA 2016
10. US National Institute of Health, *Opio*ids Report, circa 2018
11. Ibid.

Conclusion

Every republican system that has ever been established has sought to reconcile freedom with responsibility. The ability to act responsibly in accordance with the public good is called civic virtue. In Athens, Sparta, Rome, and America, there were specific requirements and expectations for citizens; the idea being, that without a civic-minded people, the society would surely crumble beneath itself. Due to the fact that the elites must bend, somewhat, to the will of the commoners, it is essential to create a society of people who strive for good, in order to establish the stability and legality that is required for the continuation of civilized society. In analyzing the Roman and American Republics, the qualities of virtuous citizens can be clearly seen, which will be juxtaposed with the lack of civic virtue in America to illustrate the consequences of deviating from this path.

Specifically, in Roman days the society established a platform for national pride. Although dissent from the government was possible, as can be seen when Cato the Younger criticized the prolonged absence of Julius Caesar from the Senate and demanded he end his military conquest, Cato's motivations were never questioned. The first virtue in Rome was that the citizens should have an eternal loyalty to the state. While one was free to express his opinions, he would never let his political party, or special interest group, interfere with the immense pride he had for his country. The "country over party" mentality eventually allowed the society to last more than four hundred years. Cicero once feared that the citizens of the republic were losing the sense of what made them Roman, hence the decline in 44 B.C. The next virtue was different depending on whether one was a man or woman. Men in Rome were guided by honor, and every decision and speech one made was in accordance with this principle. It was thought of as highly irregular to insult someone's honor in public. This belief actually derived from Plato in ancient

Greece—the most important form of a man was his public form. As a result, men in Rome would always wear their best clothes out in public, write eloquently, and speak full of vigor and verve. Women in Rome were primarily concerned with *Pudicitia*, meaning chastity, modesty, and fidelity. They were expected to act in a sexually acceptable way and never betray their husbands. The qualities of nationalism, honor, and fidelity classified one as Roman.

In the American Republic, at the time of the founding, the same Roman virtues were present in society. The society was established on timocratical ideas, meaning it was a society based on honor. In the Declaration of Independence, Jefferson concludes by writing that ". . . we mutually pledge to each other our lives, our fortunes, and our Sacred honor." More so, the early American founders stressed the importance of honesty, and to act or speak dishonestly was to betray the public's trust in you. George Washington stated that he hoped nobody dishonest would ever hold the office of the presidency. Lastly, the writing and speaking of the day was unique—everyone would constantly try to prove their intelligence and ability to others. These actions were not based on insecurity, but rather in response to a society that cultivated and respected intelligence. The qualities of honor, honesty, and intelligence defined the average American.

In the twenty-first century, Americans typically associate civic virtue with voting in elections, serving on juries, and obeying the laws. However, behaviors such as these represent the bare minimum in a republic. The expectation should be so much more. A virtuous citizen in any republic should be honest, honorable, nationalistic, intelligent, and respectful. The majority of citizens at the time of America's founding embodied these principles. However, in modern times, the people have abandoned them in pursuit of personal gain and preservation. In the words of scholar Rod Holder, "there are only two things in life that are free: air and choices." This is a reality that faces all people: choose the right path or the wrong one. The problem became exacerbated by the fact that choosing the wrong path leads to riches and personal success. If one avoids paying their taxes, they will become richer; if one cheats on a test, it will lead to a higher score. Unfortunately, people who see themselves as above such behavior are frequently mocked as being vain and arrogant. However, people who stick to more ethical avenues of behavior are doing more than simply adhering to some sense of self-righteousness—they are Preserving the Republic.

People have the ability to dictate America's cultural and political factors through their actions. Frequent drug and alcohol abuse, increased viewership in pornographic material, increased disobedience to legal codes, lack of civic participation, and widespread poor financial decisions are not the way to foster a strong Republic. When the populace adopts these behaviors on a large scale, it permits the elites to not only continue them, but to take them further. Eventually, the citizenry allowed themselves to follow the elites into the darkness . . . Today, We the People have lost our sense of what it means to be American.

The constant unethical actions of Americans have created a firmament of dishonor over the country and has led directly to the election of an absolute demagogue, President Donald Trump. In the words of Theodore Roosevelt, "The most practical kind of politics is the politics of decency." Trump has repeatedly called for the imprisonment of his political rivals, assaulted the media for accountable reporting, and lied to his millions of followers daily using his now-banned social media platform. The reality, though, is that Trump was simply a manifestation of a citizenry without civic virtue and standards of excellence. The good news is that there is hope—while the process of civic decline has begun, it can be reversed and salvaged by the populace. What is at stake is the very soul and longevity of the United States. The loyalty to country over party must be revived, the honesty and honor of all individuals must be refreshed, and the aspiring to intelligence and excellence must reconvene. The people of the U.S. are truly better than what we have demonstrated over the past few decades. This problem, truly, cannot be solved through the implementation of national policies—it begins with just one person making one decision.

Index

About the Authors

Justin P. DePlato is an expert on the American presidency and American founding theories. He has published several books focusing on many American politics topics.

Alex C. Minford graduated summa cum laude from Robert Morris University with a BA in Political Science. He has previously worked as a legislative intern in the U.S. House of Representatives, and he is now earning an MBA.

www.ingramcontent.com/pod-product-compliance
Ingram Content Group UK Ltd.
Pitfield, Milton Keynes, MK11 3LW, UK
UKHW041844031026
15587UKWH00003B/997

9 781793 62751